The Quotable Marathoner

The Quotable
Marathoner

BY CHARLES LYONS

THE LYONS PRESS
Guilford, Connecticut
An imprint of The Globe Pequot Press

The Lyons Press is an imprint of the Globe Pequot Press.

Printed in the United States of America

10 9 8 7 6 5 4 3 2 1

Design by Compset, Inc.

Library of Congress Cataloging-in-Publication Data

The quotable marathoner / [compiled] by Charles Lyons.
    p. cm.
    Includes bibliographical references and index.
    ISBN 1-58574-404-2
    1. Marathon running—Quotations, maxims, etc. 2. Runners (Sports)—Quotations. 3. Marathon running—Anecdotes. I. Lyons, Charles, 1960–

GV1065.Q68 2001
796.42'52—dc21

2001038162

Acknowledgments

Thanks are due to John Elliott of MarathonGuide. com, the members of the Web site who sent in their quotes, and to The New York Road Runner's Club.

Also, a special thanks to Joe Henderson and to all the other authors from whose writing I quote. This book would not exist without them.

I'd also like to thank Becky Koh of The Lyons Press for her expert editorial advice in preparing this book.

Contents

Introduction

"How dull it is to pause, to make an end, to rush unburnished, not to shine in use."

ALFRED LORD TENNYSON, "ULYSSES"

"If you want to run, run a mile. If you want to experience another life, run a marathon."

EMIL ZATOPEK

I'm on a plane flying back from London; it's been a busy week, filled with meetings and late nights hustling around Piccadilly to get scoops for my *Variety* articles.

I haven't run a step in six days. My legs feel like lead.

I pick up the phone to call my editor, Peter Bart, to discuss a story. I mention, casually, not bragging, that I am running the New York Marathon on Sunday. He mutters: "Now, what would you do a thing like that for, my boy?"

He's got a point.

Why would I? I have hardly trained, except for a hideously slow fifteen-miler around Hyde Park last week and those sluggish five- or seven-mile runs, three times a week and often on a treadmill, over the previous month or so. Yet as the quotations assembled in this book will attest, the decision to run a marathon is rarely logical and never fully explainable to family, friends, and co-workers.

I once asked the ultra marathoner Stu Mittleman why he runs. His answer: "You've got to move beyond the 'why' and get to the 'how.'" But most of our reasons for running are less metaphysical and more pragmatic.

For me, running marathons began as a competitive undertaking. It was a way of testing my young metal, of asserting my individuality, and sometimes of avoiding more pressing questions, such as "What do I want to do with my life?" But oddly, as I have moved away from competition toward finding more joy in running, the activity has become more vital to my well-being.

Since the late 1970s, when I took up running as an overzealous high school student, marathons have occupied a unique space in my psyche, a safe haven away from whatever travails I happen to be living through at the time.

The briskness of the fall air, even in Los Angeles, connects me to years past when I was thinner and hungrier for success at the grueling challenge. At this time, for every year over the past two decades, I come to feel it in my bones, in the bounce in my walk, in the amount of time I spend staring at the blank pages of my running log, in how often images of the start and finish line of a marathon pop into my mind.

On long training runs on misty mornings along San Vicente Boulevard, I imagine passing each of the mile marks of the course, see a large clock registering my progress toward completion. The clock does not lie. It gives me what I deserve. It is the ultimate truth-telling machine.

But success is a personal thing, and I am no authority to prattle on about it anyway. All I know is this: I have never been more sure of myself, more invigorated and more ready for all of what life has to offer than when I am training well.

It was 1978 when I first conquered Central Park's 6-mile loop on an after-school run with my high school physics teacher, Keith Francis. I was exuberant, high on my accomplishment for weeks. It wasn't long, however, before I wanted to prove I could go farther. I entered a marathon six months later, as a freshman in college. And I finished. I felt radiant with success and my confidence spread to my classwork, which suddenly appeared to get easier. I was hooked.

I didn't have the runners' lean and hungry look then, and I don't have it now. But running has become my sport, my religion, my entertainment and my medicine. It has come to serve as a complement to every part of my life.

"I know of no more encouraging fact," says Henry David Thoreau in *Walden*, "than the unquestionable ability of man to raise himself through conscious endeavor." A marathon, all 26 miles and 385 yards of it, is a distance and a way of life we choose. Most of us do so not to set records but for no other reason than our desire to better ourselves—as athletes, as people.

"Rejoice, we conquer."

Pheidippides is the Greek messenger who, myth has it, ran from the battle of Marathon to Athens to deliver news of the Greek defeat of the Persians. Upon arriving in Athens, accounts claim he said: "Rejoice, we conquer," then promptly died. Though the precise distance Pheidippides ran is believed to be close to 26 miles, the first official marathon length was the 25-mile marathon held during the first modern Olympics in Athens in 1896. During the London Olympics of 1908, the marathon as we know it became standardized at 26.2 miles, the extra 1.2 tagged on to a 25-miler so that the race could start in front of the palace for the Queen to watch.

Somehow, the odd distance adds to the marathon's appeal. For me it always serves as a reminder that, in running the marathon, I am part of history. But my own encounters with some 25 marathons—in New York, Boston, Miami, Los Angeles, Albany, NY, Foxboro, MA, and elsewhere—are less interesting than the runners' voices you are about to read. The aim of these pages is to provide a little treasure chest of words about the marathon and running. Some, I hope, will be inspiring. Some will be brutally honest reminders of the work involved in this particular form of play. Others will help you to find the connections between the running you do and the life you lead.

Divided into four chapters, the book takes you from the words of first-time marathoners to the wisdom of the masters, reflecting on the sport. In the first chapter, First Encounters, Grete Waitz, upon completing her first New York City Marathon, expresses what nearly everyone has after their first battle with the beast: "I'll never do that again." Waitz was a world-class track runner from Norway when the late New York Runners Club president, Fred Lebow, persuaded her to run through the streets of the Big Apple. Not only would she do it again, she would do it all over the world, quite often, for years to come, becoming one of the most famous names in the sport and a pioneer for women's distance running worldwide.

In Training, you will read quotations from the likes of Jeff Galloway, Joan Benoit Samuelson, Hal Higdon, George Sheehan, James Fixx, Juma Ikangaa, Billy Rogers, John "The Penguin" Bingham, and Gordon Bakoulis; all are experts in the art of preparing the body for the grueling challenge. "Everyone is an athlete," says Sheehan, whose many books on running are among the most thoughtful ever written. "The only difference is that some of us are in training, some not." Galloway, who ran on the 1972 Olympic Marathon team with Frank Shorter and become an authority on marathon training, has slowed down over the years. But intentionally. "I spent the first twenty years of my running career trying to run as many miles as I could as fast as I could," he writes. "Then I spent the next twenty years trying to figure out how to run the least amount of miles needed to finish a marathon." And the lithe Tanzanian legend Ikangaa's statement, "The will to win means nothing without the will to prepare," reminds us all that we create our marathon race every time we lace up our sneakers and head out the door.

Racing takes you to the starting line and into the heads and hearts of some of the luminaries and everyday runners who have traversed marathons in Boston, New York, and around the country. You will meet such runners as Johnny Kelly, Tom Fleming, Frank Shorter, Alberto Salazar, Rod Dixon, Rob de Castella, Clarence DeMar, and Uta Pippig, not to mention the Czech phenomenon, Emil Zatopek. "Men, today we die a little," Zatopek said on the starting line of the 1952 Helsinki Olympic Marathon, a race he would win. Years later, Australian marathon great Rob de Castella opined about the marathon race: "If you feel bad at 10 miles, you're in trouble. If you feel bad at 20 miles, you're normal. If you don't feel bad at 26 miles, you're abnormal."

Reflections includes quotations from such reflective souls as Joe Henderson, *The Joy of Running* author Thaddeus Kostrubala, *The Zen of Running* author Fred Rohe, James Fixx, Pricilla Welch, and Japanese coach Kiyoshi Nakamura. Kostrubala in particular preaches in no uncertain terms the long-term emotional, spiritual, and physical benefits of running in general and marathoning in particular. "I feel that slow long-distance running is not a sport at all," he writes. "It is an activity that resonates with our biological heritage. And, in so resonating, we may be able to penetrate the confines of our circumstance and establish a better harmony with ourselves and our world."

Quotes such as these inspire me as I hope they do you. If you haven't run a marathon yet, maybe these quotes will intrigue you to take up the sport that can change the quality of your life and also extend it. If nothing else, I hope the quotes enable you to better understand what drives thousands of people every year to pursue and defeat the marathon.

I have found training for and racing marathons to be a path toward a healthier, more productive, less stressful, more romantic, and more deeply contemplative life. I hope the words in this book help you find the marathoner in you.

Los Angeles, CA
February 2001

First Encounters

"I was so depleted of energy, food and fluids, there was nothing left inside but a wonderful, awesome, total feeling of accomplishment."

LEAH BOGG IN *FIRST MARATHONS*

I wish I could fully remember my first marathon. It was in the fall of 1978, in Livermore, California, of that I'm sure. The leaves were changing colors. The course traversed a winery, or several. I was wearing a blue cotton shirt and I ran the entire race with a school friend with whom I had been training.

We ran stride for stride. He was better than I, but the point was to do this race together. I was 18, he 19.

Little did I know that 22 years later, I would still be hooked on marathoning.

I cannot remember my splits or whether I walked at all during the race. I don't think there were many course spectators or water stops. I remember a long straight-away and finally seeing the finish line, then racing toward it for 220 yards at breakneck speed, holding hands with my running partner at the finish. Next I remember chugging cups upon cups of water. Then there was the muscle soreness and the limping to get attention.

I also remember crying. Not out of sadness but from joy. I could finally turn off the stress. The race was an exorcism that will stay with me forever. It whetted my appetite for the running life—as I think all first marathons do.

"I'll never do that again."

GRETE WAITZ, ON FIRST RUNNING THE NYC MARATHON IN 1978

———•·•·•———

"I ran my first marathon in 1990 through the five boroughs of New York. Being a native New Yorker, it was without a doubt one of the most rewarding moments of my life. In his song 'Heroes,' David Bowie sings, 'We can be heroes! Just for one day.' Participating in the New York Marathon made me feel like a hero. But the wonderful thing about the NYC Marathon is that you don't necessarily have to be a runner to be a participant. The millions of spectators and the thousands of volunteers, who make us runners feel like heroes, are themselves heroes. Because of this, every first Sunday in November, New York City truly becomes a city of heroes."

KEVIN MCALLISTER, WARREN STREET SOCIAL AND ATHLETIC CLUB, BRONX, NY

"I had been running in the Palos Verdes Marathon at a 6:00-minute mile pace. My shoelaces came undone at 2 miles and finally I decided to stop and tie my shoes, and as we all know my muscles all tightened so that I had to basically painfully walk the last 11 miles. I was in such pain at the end, I promised myself I'd never again run a marathon. It took me 22 years to break that promise."

ARNOLD ROSS, LOS ANGELES, CA

"My biggest piece of advice to first-time marathoners: enjoy yourself and have fun. Most people can't believe I would put fun and marathon in the same sentence, but training is the difficult part. The marathon is the reward for all the months of hard work and sacrifice."

MELISSA MCCARTHY, WARREN STREET ATHLETIC CLUB, LAMBERTVILLE, NJ

"You have to go at your own pace. Egos can't be involved. That's exactly how it is in life, too."

BONNIE BROWN, AFTER COMPLETING
THE LOS ANGELES MARATHON, MARCH 2001

"I've only run one marathon. That sounds defeatist in nature now that I read it. One marathon is 100 percent more than most of the people on the face of the Earth have run."

DARRIN DOLEHANTY, RICHMOND, IN

"I completed my first marathon a couple of years ago and liked it so much I recently completed my 5th! Just an ordinary marathoner, walker . . . seven hours!"

LISA LACHANCE, LOS GATOS, CA

"On my first marathon: Grandfather Mt. Boone, North Carolina. I could see the top as I reached mile 25. The last 1.2 would be the easiest. I knew it! Since then my marathon mantra has been: O, those first 25. So easy to be alive."

KEN DELANO, ASHEVILLE, NC

"When I began training for my first marathon [Chicago, 1999], my biggest fear was not whether or not I would finish, but that I would be the heaviest person at the starting line and I was not at all overweight! I quickly discovered that people of all sizes, ages and walks of life run marathons. There is no such thing as a stereotypical marathoner. That makes marathon running even more appealing to me!"

AMANDA MUSACCHIO, VILLA PARK, IL

"While I was out there running, I was thinking about people who can't do this. Just be thankful that you have the opportunity to do it and are not in a wheelchair at home. At 24 miles, I felt close to God."

RICK FLORES, AFTER COMPLETING THE LOS ANGELES MARATHON, MARCH 2001

—————

"I am a blind runner, having started at age 40 in 1988 with no training, by walking the LA Marathon with my guide dog. In 1992, I acquired a treadmill and with it and friends in two running clubs, I've progressed from walking to running and have a PR of 4:39 in San Francisco. Bagpipe music gives me more adrenalin for longer than all the power bars and gels combined."

SHARLENE WILLS, LOS ANGELES, CA

"I don't know which was more compelling: the fact that I had accomplished my goal, or that I was part of this amazing demonstration of the human willpower."

HEIDI L. WINSLOW BUTTS IN *FIRST MARATHONS*

"Sometimes it's just surreal out there, while you're running a marathon. People standing out in the rain cheering for you, people blasting music for you. It's an awesome show of camaraderie and community."

JOHN ROBERTS, AFTER COMPLETING THE LOS ANGELES MARATHON, MARCH 2001

"I ran the LA Marathon in 1999 . . . The fact is I planned on finishing the race and I did. The reality was I almost fainted afterwards and needed a fluid IV. No fun. And the pain afterwards: I could hardly walk for over one week. This year I have been training consistently and can't wait for race day!"

CHRISTINE WIKA, WOODLAND HILLS, CA

—•••—

"You will never have another first marathon. Don't worry about your finishing time. Relax and enjoy the event."

JUDY WATKINS, RRCA COACH, FT. LAUDERDALE, FL

"As I was running the last five miles of my first marathon [an out and back], I was watching the runners next to me. All seemed like soldiers returning to base from a mission. A mission accomplished. Defeating the marathon."

JAN TEUTSCH, TEL AVIV, ISRAEL

"My first marathon was the Twin Cities in October. It was a beautiful run. The last four miles were tough, but the training program I did only had you run a max of 18 miles. Next time I'll do at least 21 or 22. . . . Keep your head up high and reach for the sky. Anything you want is within your reach, along with your shoes."

JANET GARDIN, ROSEVILLE, MN

"My most memorable thought when I was about three-fourths the way through the race [around mile 19] had to do with convincing myself that I wasn't about to disappoint my family or especially myself, after all the time I spent preparing myself to get here. By repeatedly telling myself that statement I was able to continue to push ahead and finish strong. The mind really does have miraculous power over the body."

JIM THOELKE, KENNEWICK, WA

————

"In April of 2000, I read an article about people starting to run marathons in their forties. I heard a voice in my soul telling me to do it. Run a marathon!"

STEPHEN RUE, NEW ORLEANS, LA

"Around mile 24, I ran into one of the girls again. She seemed to be struggling. I think we were all struggling a little by that time, but without any words, she just grabbed my hand . . . for just a moment. I told her that she was almost there and that she was going to make it. So many times I wanted to quit, or at least let my group run ahead but they would not let that happen."

ALISON RIBACK, FINISHER, 2000 CHICAGO MARATHON

"My advice to first-time marathoners is to expect the unexpected on the big day. During my 6 months of training I never experienced leg cramps but on marathon day I developed severe leg cramps at mile 5 and ran with them for the next 10 miles. At mile 15, I had to make a stop at the porta potty and had about a 4 to 5 minute walk. After leaving the porta potty, I realized that I could barely walk and had to tell my partner to go on. Here is the lesson I learned: if you find yourself with leg cramps on your big day, you must keep moving . . ."

BRIAN SPRADLEY, FORT WORTH, TX

"When I turned 41, I realized I was running out of time. I realized I needed to do something significant. This was my Mt. Everest."

STEVE BATHGATE, AFTER COMPLETING THE LOS ANGELES MARATHON, MARCH 2001

"I am a 30-year-old mother of three children, all of whom are under the age of four. I just completed my first marathon. . . . During the race, I kept repeating to myself that if I could give birth three times, I could certainly run a marathon. Guess what? Running a marathon is a lot easier than having a baby and almost as rewarding!"

LEIGH DEFAZIO, FINISHER OF THE 2001 LAS VEGAS
INTERNATIONAL MARATHON

"Crossing the finish line at my first marathon was like ending one life and starting another. Now I was a runner. A whole new world opened up to me."

WAYNE GIBBONS IN *FIRST MARATHONS*

"On a training run, Leon Kupersmit had a massive heart attack and passed away. He was only 53. At his funeral, one of his sons buried Leon with his New York City Marathon finisher's medal. We all love Leon and miss him very much. Many of Leon's friends from the training group had planned to run the Houston Marathon, so I decided to join them and run in memory of Leon. Despite my injured knee and slower time, Leon and I finished the marathon together. He was with me in mind and spirit the entire way."

STEPHEN RUE, NEW ORLEANS, LA

"In retrospect, running and racing 26.2 miles has taught me an important lesson in life. The lesson is that I am in control at every mile of the 26.2-mile race. I decide whether or not to stop, slow down or pick up the pace. In life, outside of running, I am also in total control of my life. I control who I am, where I am, where I am going, where I will be and who I will become."

M. SUE BOZGOZ, FAYETTEVILLE, GA

"To run a marathon, you must begin the race with the idea that you will finish it. As the miles go by in the race, and I begin to feel tired, I begin a rhythmic chant [a mantra], in order for my mind to stay occupied. So, with 6 miles to go, I may say: 'Six more miles, way to go,' rhythmically. I first started this during the Charlotte Observer Marathon and I had my PR of 3:29."

STEVE GOULD, RICHMOND, VA

"The first thing I did was tell everyone I knew that I was training for a marathon. This was my way of guaranteeing that I would run it and not back down. After I made such a bragging fool of myself, I had to run!"

JIM MILLER IN *FIRST MARATHONS*

"This marathon was harder than I thought. I trained a lot of 20 milers that were easier than this. The last few miles were the hardest thing in my life. It's a matter of forcing your body to keep moving when it's out of resources. A half hour from now, I know I will feel that all the work has paid off."

BILL RABKIN, AFTER COMPLETING THE LOS ANGELES MARATHON, MARCH 2001

"Running that first marathon so many years ago opened a new door for me. Instead of retiring from the sport as I had previously planned, I was reborn as a road runner and enjoyed another decade of success. During that time, I was joined by millions of others who found themselves similarly reborn through road running."

GRETE WAITZ IN *THE NEW YORK ROAD RUNNERS CLUB COMPLETE BOOK OF RUNNING AND FITNESS*

———•◆•———

"For the last six months we'd been trying to explain to friends or coworkers why we wanted to run a marathon. Now we were in a crowd of people who understood why. There was no need to explain. I loved being a part of them, of their energy. I felt like I belonged there."

KIM AHRENS IN *FIRST MARATHONS*

"A first marathon is like a first love. You might bumble through it, but you never forget. Nothing you do later will ever be quite as memorable as your initiation, even if its memories are painful."

JOE HENDERSON, *MARATHON TRAINING*

———

"Time as a goal becomes irrelevant for someone attempting a marathon. The only goal worth considering for first-time marathoners is the finish line."

HAL HIGDON, *MARATHON: THE ULTIMATE TRAINING GUIDE*

———

"My completing a marathon, I feel like I can take on anything. It's very relaxing and reassuring to the mind. There's no better feeling in the world, to push yourself to the limit and beyond."

GARY ROBERTSON, AFTER COMPLETING THE LOS ANGELES MARATHON, MARCH 2001

"I don't really like to run. Doing it for five hours and 12 minutes made that even worse. But it's a challenge and it proved very worthwhile. Plus I got to do it with my brother."

SCOTT SHERMAN, AFTER COMPLETING THE LOS ANGELES MARATHON, MARCH 2001

Training

"Don't let the planning and analyzing get in the way of the doing and enjoying."

JOE HENDERSON

When I started researching this book, my weight had crept up to around 210 lbs. I had been using alcohol as a tool for escaping my own frustrations. It wasn't serious drinking, but it was a habit that was slowly causing me to lose sight of my goals. My writing goals. My athletic goals. And most importantly, my goal to become a better person.

I instinctively knew something must be done. I went back to New York over the holidays, saw family, and began reconstructing my life. I started caring about everything I put into my body. I stopped going out, stopped drinking. I took up yoga. I began breathing better.

It was chiefly running that grounded me again. I didn't have any other goal than to get myself back into shape. No races planned. No logbook. No mileage fanaticism. No guilty feelings if I took a day off. I needed to rediscover the joy of running and in so doing rediscover the joy of life.

In a couple of months, as I read more and more about running and deliberated which quotations to use for this book, I began to re-embrace the sport's restorative powers. Not only was I looking trimmer, but also I was feeling better about everything and I saw, through running and fitness and body care, the clear path toward a better life.

I now run 3 to 4 times a week, putting in at least one challenging run. I have never felt better. The New York Marathon swims around in my mind as a possible next goal, but, having run it several times already, I don't feel compelled. If the hunger comes, I will respond.

Training for a marathon is a rewarding goal, and there are specific steps one needs to take to achieve it, but the greater reward is often what the process of training can bring to everyday life.

Training enables one to set priorities. To live more fully. To be a better person to those around you. I used to slack off most of the year and then cram train for specific marathons; later I would wonder why I hadn't done better. Not a wise approach. Be sure that the goal that you set for yourself does not cause you to lose sight of this process, this activity, this pleasure, this lifestyle choice.

"Somewhere in the world there is someone training when you are not. When you race him, he will win."

TOM FLEMING IN *BOSTON MARATHON* BY TOM DERDERIAN

———◦•◦•◦———

"One runner asks the other, 'How many runners do you think are out running this early?' Answer: 'Frankie, all those runners that finish before us in the race, they got out here before we did.'"

KENNETH HARKLESS, BESSEMER, AL

———◦•◦•◦———

"Training is not only a means, it is also an end in itself."

GEORGE SHEEHAN IN *THE NEW YORK ROAD RUNNERS CLUB COMPLETE BOOK OF RUNNING AND FITNESS*

"Rest is always necessary for the body to recover and re-plenish itself. Furthermore, the light days will allow more work in training sessions on the hard days, giving greater progress in the long run."

BILL BOWERMAN, 1972 U.S. OLYMPIC TEAM COACH,
IN *MAKE YOUR OWN TIME*

"It no longer takes an injury for me to incorporate rest and recovery into my training schedule . . . rest is a component as important in my schedule as speedwork or a long run."

JOAN BENOIT SAMUELSON, *THE RUNNING TIMES GUIDE TO BREAKTHROUGH RUNNING*

"The marathon is 26 miles, 385 yards. I don't know of anyone who can run that distance without training. And the training is a slow, gradual buildup of the body, by slow long-distance running, to be able to run that distance."

THADDEUS KOSTRUBALA, *THE JOY OF RUNNING*

"Because they are prepared, most trained marathoners finish. Rarely does an unprepared person make it past 20 miles."

F. C. FREDERICK, "THE RUNNING BODY," IN *MAKE YOUR OWN TIME*

"You've got to make up your mind. You've got to be determined . . . you've got to have strong motivation. It has to almost be an obsession."

WALTER STACK, ON RUNNING MARATHONS AFTER AGE 70,
IN *MARATHON RUNNERS*

"Everyone is an experiment of one."

GEORGE SHEEHAN IN *RUNNER'S WORLD COMPLETE BOOK OF RUNNING*

———•••———

"Your body, no matter how you train it, is only capable of standing so much stress, then you have to let it rest."

FRANK SHORTER IN *OUTSIDE* MAGAZINE

———•••———

"You have to believe in the training effect, the astonishing physiological principle that says the organism improves in response to stress."

JOHN JEROME, *THE ELEMENTS OF EFFORT*

"You have to be a little bored to be doing really good training."

MARTY LIQUORI IN *RUNNERS AND OTHER DREAMERS*

———•••———

"Remind yourself in your training that you are out there to make yourself happy. Challenging yourself will be part of the process."

GORDON BAKOULIS BLOCH, *HOW TO TRAIN FOR AND RUN YOUR BEST MARATHON*

———•••———

"Base training—that is, pure aerobic training—should compose the bulk of any distance runner's training."

MARK CONOVER, *THE RUNNING TIMES GUIDE TO BREAKTHROUGH RUNNING*

"We must train, it seems, especially when our life gets a little fat, our soul a little out of shape."

RICHARD HARTEIS, *MARATHON: A STORY OF ENDURANCE AND FRIENDSHIP*

"Marathon training is roughly analogous to taking large doses of medication for an infection and continuing the medication after the infection has disappeared."

MARK BLOOM, *THE MARATHON: WHAT IT TAKES TO GO THE DISTANCE*

"When you mentally 'tough it out' in rehearsal, over and over, it's easier to 'gut it out' in the marathon itself."

JEFF GALLOWAY, *MARATHON*

"Training for a marathon is much like climbing a ladder. Each ring is a short-term goal that must be met in sequence in order to reach the long-term goal at the top of the ladder."

RICHARD BENYO, *MAKING THE MARATHON YOUR EVENT*

"The distance runner must develop endurance speed— the ability to sustain a quick pace comfortably."

BROOKS JOHNSON IN *THE RUNNING TIMES GUIDE TO BREAKTHROUGH RUNNING*

"I've done training routines when every outing meant excruciating pain—buying into the notion that 'good training' must be uncomfortable. But that's just not true. All you really need to be is consistent."

ALBERTO SALAZAR, *ALBERTO SALAZAR'S GUIDE TO RUNNING*

"The most important piece of equipment is your shoes."

DAVE KUEHLS, *4 MONTHS TO A 4 HOUR MARATHON*

"You have to remember one thing. The only thing that separates the runner from the road is the shoe. So the importance of shoes is tremendous. If you don't have the proper shoe, you're going to get injured."

DR. ANDRES RODRIGUEZ IN *THE ESSENTIAL RUNNER*

"Excessive upper-body rotation wastes energy as the top half twists above the hips much like a washing machine agitator swishing back and forth."

ROY BENSON IN *RUNNING TIMES GUIDE TO BREAKTHROUGH RUNNING*

"If you're feeling rundown, convince yourself that it won't hurt to take a day or two off—or even to reduce your training for an entire week. The alternative is a lot worse."

ALBERTO SALAZAR, *ALBERTO SALAZAR'S GUIDE TO RUNNING*

———

"When running in cold weather, follow the old rule of dressing in several light-weight layers rather than one heavy garment."

TERESA GIBREAL, *THE RUNNING TIMES GUIDE TO BREAKTHROUGH RUNNING*

———

"It's just developing the attitude that nothing can stop you."

RON HILL, 2:09 MARATHONER, IN *MAKE YOUR OWN TIME*

"Monitoring your body while training for a marathon is a little like teaching yourself how to write. You have to pay attention to what is being played out, listen to your instincts, make the subconscious conscious."

RICHARD HARTEIS, *MARATHON: A STORY OF ENDURANCE AND FRIENDSHIP*

"Become proficient at listening to your body and you will eventually hear from your totality—the complex, unique person you are."

GEORGE SHEEHAN IN *DR. GEORGE SHEEHAN ON RUNNING*

"Overtraining is a simple trap."

ALBERTO SALAZAR, *ALBERTO SALAZAR'S GUIDE TO RUNNING*

"You have within you, right now, all that you need to achieve your realistic goals in running. Thinking like a champion will allow you to reach that potential. Remember that all your accomplishments are the direct result of your thoughts. When you choose the right kind of thoughts, you can create the running destiny you have always wanted."

AMBY BURFOOT IN *RUNNER'S WORLD COMPLETE BOOK OF RUNNING*

"If you can stick to the training throughout the many long years, then willpower is no longer a problem. It's raining? That doesn't matter. I am tired? That's besides the point. It's simply that I just have to."

EMIL ZATOPEK IN *EARTH'S TEARING CRY AND HEAVEN'S BEARING SMILE* BY SRI CHINMOY

"Each run is an end in itself. Just being there experiencing it is enough."

GARY ELLIOTT, ALLISON ROE'S COACH AND CO-AUTHOR OF *EVERY RUNNER'S COMPANION*

"A beginning runner can reasonably increase endurance by about 15 minutes every week."

DAVE KUEHLS, *4 MONTHS TO A 4 HOUR MARATHON*

"In all cases, be responsive. Develop an awareness of your body, its needs and capacities. Coax a slow, continuous stream of adaptations out of it. If you are deligent and sensitive, training will progress and you will avoid injury."

F. C. FREDERICK, "THE RUNNING BODY," IN *MAKE YOUR OWN TIME*

"If you're after improvement in yourself—it doesn't matter what level you're at—the first thing you've got to do is to be aware of yourself. . . . Know your capabilities."

GARY ELLIOTT, ALLISON ROE'S COACH AND CO-AUTHOR OF *EVERY RUNNER'S COMPANION*

"Everyone is an athlete. The only difference is that some of us are in training, some not."

GEORGE SHEEHAN IN *HEROES AND SPARROWS: A CELEBRATION OF RUNNING* BY ROGER ROBINSON

"I run until I can't run anymore. And then I run some more."

EMIL ZATOPEK, SAID IN 1952, WHEN HE WON TRIPLE VICTORIES AT THE HELSINKI OLYMPICS

"Consistent training will make you an excellent runner. Training every day will make you an excellent golfer."

LEAH BACH, BURNABY, BC

"I spent the first twenty years of my running career trying to run as many miles as I could as fast as I could. Then I spent the next twenty years trying to figure out how to run the least amount of miles needed to finish a marathon. And I've come to the conclusion the second way is much more enjoyable."

JEFF GALLOWAY, 1972 OLYMPIAN, IN *FIRST MARATHONS*

"Marathon runners mainly want to finish . . . Marathon racers want to improve."

JOE HENDERSON, *MAKE YOUR OWN TIME*

"I know the marathon is impossible. It is impossible physically and spiritually. I am afraid of it. I can't drive the course ahead of time in a car. It's too long. No one can run that far. Two years ago I couldn't run 100 yards. I was fat. I still feel fat. I think fat. The scale says I weigh 175 pounds. I see 230. I feel 300."

THADDEUS KOSTRUBALA, *THE JOY OF RUNNING*

"Five minutes of discipline—that's all it takes. When you get up in the morning, hit the head, pull on your stuff and get out the door. Everything else just falls into place."

PAUL FETSCHER, WARREN STREET ATHLETIC CLUB, NEW YORK, NY

"The long run is the key. Skimp on weekly short runs, but devote yourself to the long one."

LENNARD DAVIS, BRONX, NY

"The long run is the single most important ingredient to marathon success."

BOB GLOVER IN *THE NEW YORK ROAD RUNNERS CLUB COMPLETE BOOK OF RUNNING AND FITNESS*

"Use the long run to its fullest. Ask yourself, 'Where do I hurt after the run? What muscles are sore? Do I feel dehydrated? What about my shoes; were they laced too tight? Did I wear the right socks?' Use it as a form of self-assessment."

STU MITTLEMAN IN *THE ESSENTIAL MARATHONER*

"Cross train once or twice a week."

DAVE KUEHLS, *4 MONTHS TO A 4 HOUR MARATHON*

"In general, any form of exercise, if pursued continuously, will help to train us in perseverance. Long-distance running is particularly good."

MAO TSE-TUNG

———•••••———

"You're bound to have days when everything seems sluggish and ungainly and you'd just as soon not be training at all. That's a good time to persist."

JAMES FIXX, THE COMPLETE BOOK OF RUNNING

———•••••———

"Physical training is only ten percent of the total preparation; the ninety is mental."

KIYOSHI NAKAMURA, JAPANESE MARATHONER TOSHIHIKO SEKO'S SENSEI, IN THE MASTERS OF THE MARATHON

"Sometimes it's an incredible drag. Just yesterday I went out and ran about twenty-three miles and I was swearing at people and hitting mailboxes. I didn't want to be out there but I knew I had to. I'd say most runners half-like and half-dislike running."

BILL ROGERS IN *THE BOSTON MARATHON* BY JOE FALLS

———

"Goal setting is not a mind game. It is a process of developing the internal willpower to accomplish what you have set out to do."

JOAN BENOIT SAMUELSON, *RUNNING FOR WOMEN*

"I still love those long runs on Sundays. They're the mainstay of any training program. You don't get results immediately. It's like saving pennies. Put them in a jar, and at first it doesn't seem as though you have much. But after a few months, the volume begins to look impressive."

ROBERT WALLACE IN *RUNNER'S WORLD COMPLETE BOOK OF RUNNING*

"Ultimately, you have to go by what you feel. If you've planned a long run but realized after ten miles that you've had it, it's better to stop and leave it for another time. Listen to your body to see how your muscles react to the run. That's also the best way to avoid injury. Progress regularly, and if you find it difficult, stop and choose a more gradual course of progression."

JACQUELINE GAREAU, 1980 WOMEN'S BOSTON MARATHON WINNER, IN *THE COMPLETE RUNNER*, VOL. 2

"The key to running a good marathon is to not listen to anyone's advice the last week before the race. That's when people tend to do stupid things that disrupt all the input and training of the previous months."

DON KARDONG, 4TH PLACE, 1976 OLYMPIC MARATHON, IN *FIRST MARATHONS*

"You can't cram for the final. By that, I mean you're not going to get any fitter during the last couple of weeks before the race. So don't try cramming any last minute long runs or extra training. The best thing you can do for your body is rest."

GORDON BAKOULIS BLOCH IN *THE ESSENTIAL MARATHONER*

"The will to win is nothing without the will to prepare."

JUMA IKANGAA IN *RUNNING WITH THE LEGENDS*

"Chart your progress by your own standards, and don't drive yourself too hard seeking to match somebody else's."

ALBERTO SALAZAR, *ALBERTO SALAZAR'S GUIDE TO RUNNING*

"I don't think the total mileage is very important. To me, it was the way in which I ran those miles which was important."

DEREK CLAYTON IN *THE COMPLETE RUNNER*, VOL. 2

"It's the effort that matters on the hard days."

STEVE JONES, FORMER MARATHON WORLD RECORD HOLDER, IN *RUNNING WITH THE LEGENDS*

"It's easy, once you get rolling, to keep doing more and more. The momentum just builds. But before long you get compulsive about it and start thinking that if you miss a workout, you're going to turn into a pumpkin; or worse—your racing edge is going to disappear. I think that's a lot of garbage."

HERM ATKINS, 2:11 MARATHONER, IN *THE COMPLETE RUNNER*, VOL. 2

"Training is like putting money in the bank. You deposit money, and then you can take it out. When you train, you deposit your daily miles. The more training you put in, the more money you have in the bank. But you can only expect results based on the training you put in. In other words, you can't take money out of the bank that you don't have. You can't overdraw. That's what over-racing is about. A lot of us have had that experience."

FRED LEBOW, *THE NEW YORK ROAD RUNNERS CLUB COMPLETE BOOK OF RUNNING AND FITNESS*

"Every day gives you an opportunity to improve. With every run, you can try to be better. Not just a better runner, but a better person."

JOHN "THE PENGUIN" BINGHAM, *THE COURAGE TO START*

"Think positive. You are a special person. Reward yourself with self-praise as you achieve each interim goal en route to the marathon."

HAL HIGDON, *MARATHON: THE ULTIMATE TRAINING GUIDE*

"Physical training takes place at the level of the cell. That's why nothing in training is more important than patience."

JOHN JEROME, *THE ELEMENTS OF EFFORT*

"You don't need to be fast! What you do need is will: the will to abide by a training program. The will to get up a couple of hours earlier on Saturday and Sunday morning to get your long run in. The will to structure your life a bit more over the next few months: to get more sleep, drink more fluids, eat more carefully."

JOHN HANC, *THE ESSENTIAL MARATHONER*

"The key to making a commitment you can keep is to be realistic. It also helps if you ease your way gradually into a program that advances slowly enough to leave you eager for more rather than dreading each workout."

ALBERTO SALAZAR, *ALBERTO SALAZAR'S GUIDE TO RUNNING*

"I tend to set up race situations. Usually they will be fairly realistic ones. But towards the end of an interval workout I will try to focus in as if I were running a race right at that moment. I practice race type concentration, but without setting up scenarios."

FRANK SHORTER IN *RUNNERS AND OTHER DREAMERS*

"More races are lost by training too long, too fast, or too often, than by running too short, too slow, or too seldom."

JOE HENDERSON, *MARATHON TRAINING*

"There's a great advantage in training under unfavorable conditions."

EMIL ZATOPEK

"Don't fear or fight the uphills. To use a driving or biking term, downshift into a slower climbing gear on the ascent. Then resume normal speed on the other side."

JOE HENDERSON IN *THE ESSENTIAL MARATHONER*

"The marathon is an obsession. It has to be."

MARK BLOOM, *THE MARATHON: WHAT IT TAKES TO GO THE DISTANCE*

"The marathon is a contest between your will and your resources."

JEFF GALLOWAY, *MARATHON*

"The hard part isn't the work. It's knowing what not to do, and why, and for how long—then heeding those limits."

JOE HENDERSON, *MARATHON TRAINING*

"The more you frame the marathon as a stressful experience, the more negative messages you'll receive. But it's just as easy to frame it as a positively challenging journey."

JEFF GALLOWAY, *MARATHON*

"As you train, many questions will be directed your way: What are you doing? Why are you doing it? How does it feel? What do you hope to gain? By responding in a way that emphasizes fun, improving your health, and meeting a goal, you can inspire others to follow your lead."

GORDON BAKOULIS BLOCH, *HOW TO TRAIN FOR AND RUN YOUR BEST MARATHON*

———

"I don't think they give any rewards for workouts."

CRAIG VIRGIN IN *MARATHON: THE ULTIMATE TRAINING GUIDE*

Racing

"The marathon can humble you."

BILL ROGERS

I'm one of those guys who has a tendency to run better in a workout than in a race. I am not sure why this is. Perhaps I psych myself out. Perhaps I don't concentrate well enough. Perhaps I am scared of stress, of competition. Who knows?

But I do know this: during my best marathons, I feel relaxed, as though I am not working my body at the limit. My breathing is natural and free. The splits might not be ideal or good enough for a Personal Best (PB) but they are not bad either—6:06, 6:08, 6:07. I am in a groove, pacing myself off of someone else or running so evenly that others are pacing off me.

That's what happened in New York in 1987. My training with the Warren Street Athletic Club had paid off. Building up my anaerobic threshold on a regular diet of 1.5-mile repeats around Central Park's lower loop, which we called "death loops," made me ready to take on the monster. Combined with my weekly long runs, such training transformed the idea of racing the marathon into performing a sonata that I had practiced over and over.

The lesson I learned from that experience, which I take with me in races when I am not nearly as well prepared, is to be patient. "Running a successful marathon is an exercise in holding back," says Gordon Bakoulis Bloch in her useful book *How to Train for and Run Your Best Marathon.*

My friend Ibra Morales says, "Too many people think about 26 miles and they panic. My philosophy has always been—run one mile at a time and enjoy each mile." He's right. We are doing this race for ourselves. Why not enjoy it?

Still, the tendency is to run too fast at the start, not to prepare for the fact that the marathon really only begins at the wall. "Some people say the marathon does not begin until 20 miles," Billy Rogers tells us. "That's when you hit the wall. The real truth is that the first few miles are the most important ones of the race. People who make mistakes in the early miles by going out too hard or by not taking enough water are the ones who aren't going to win the race, or, perhaps, even finish it."

One of my favorite quotations in this section comes from John "The Penguin" Bingham: "Moments before, we were mere mortals," he writes. "Now, standing proudly in front of the mirror, checking to see that the number is straight and properly place, we are warriors. . . . Like all great warriors, we stand ready to face the enemy. In most cases, that enemy is ourselves."

"I love the sense of pushing myself in the marathon. When you want to quit, stay with it. Don't let the little things let you down."

BILL STEINAUER, 70, AFTER COMPLETING THE LOS ANGELES MARATHON, MARCH 2001

"Successful marathoners must lose their cool, and allow this irrational, animal consciousness to take over."

BILL ROGERS IN *MARATHONING*

"For all of us, the miracle isn't that we finish, the miracle is that we have the courage to start."

JOHN "THE PENGUIN" BINGHAM, *THE COURAGE TO START*

"You have to dig deep inside, to get at what's all you. Your body is out of energy but you just have to push through it."

DAN MORIHIKO, AFTER COMPLETING THE LOS ANGELES MARATHON, MARCH 2001

"It's the training that gets you to the starting line. It's the pacing and energy management that gets you to the finish line."

KENNETH HARKLESS, BESSEMER, AL

"The marathon is the ultimate endurance test. Oh sure, people sometimes go longer than that. But 26 miles 385 yards is where racing ends and where ludicrous extremes begin."

JOE HENDERSON, *JOG, RUN, RACE*

"I was glad to hear my name called so many times. But in my heart, I knew the support of the crowd would do me no good. They couldn't feel what I was feeling. I was blistered and getting dizzy, and, worst of all, that empty feeling of exhaustion and fatigue was striking already."

BILL ROGERS, REFLECTING ON THE HALF-WAY POINT OF THE 1977 BOSTON MARATHON, A RACE HE WOULD NOT FINISH, IN "THE MARATHON CAN ALWAYS HUMBLE YOU" IN *BOSTON: AMERICA'S OLDEST MARATHON*

"'Hey, lady, this is Boston. Pick it up,' someone in the crowd shouted as I ran a sluggish 10-minute mile pace, closing on mile 16."

DOLORES E. CROSS, *BREAKING THROUGH THE WALL*

"You have to understand this about the start of the Boston Marathon. It's not really a start. It's a survival lesson. You should train for it by taking a karate class. If you could file your elbows to a point it would help. And forget trying to swing your arms. Throw punches."

JOHN ROMERO, "BACK AMONG THE LEGIONS," IN *BOSTON: AMERICA'S OLDEST MARATHON*

"My spirit began to ricochet off the walls and leap into the trees, but all I could bring myself to do physically by way of celebration was give a single high-pitched burst of a laugh."

RICHARD HARTEIS, ON PASSING THE 20-MILE MARK IN THE MARATHON, IN *MARATHON: A STORY OF ENDURANCE AND FRIENDSHIP*

"Diverting the mind to something not connected with the act of running, something outside the body, is used for relaxation during the first third of the marathon and during the last third, to give moments of relief from pain."

THOMAS BARRETT AND ROBERT MORRISSEY, *MARATHON RUNNERS*

———

"My goal is to run as fast as I can, but that's sort of a misnomer. It's not that I'm running as fast as I can, but that I'm covering the distance in the shortest amount of time possible. To do that in a marathon you're almost holding back for the first ten miles. It requires an almost infinite amount of patience . . . The better you know yourself, the better you're able to deal out and not waste anything. And be as efficient as possible."

JACK FULTZ, AFTER HIS 4TH PLACE FINISH OF THE BOSTON MARATHON IN 1976, IN "THE RHYME OF THE UNKNOWN MARATHONER" BY BOB MORIARTY IN *BOSTON: AMERICA'S OLDEST MARATHON*

"You can actually suffer a little bit more going slowly than when you're going really fast. A faster marathon might even be easier than a slow one, in terms of what it takes out of you mentally."

FRANK SHORTER IN *THE QUOTABLE RUNNER*

———

"Pain will ricochet around your legs and feet, evading your ice packs and stretches; doubts will invade your confidence, eroding your determination. Your feet will sprout blisters, your toenails will turn black with the blood that wells up beneath them; you will wonder sometimes what the point is, but you might as well ask about life. As far as you know, there isn't one."

JOHN HANC, *THE ESSENTIAL MARATHONER*

"Pain is sudden and sharp. Such pain does not exist in a marathon . . . what does exist in a marathon is discomfort. And fatigue. And the feeling that you are not having a very good day. And the feeling that you have been running a long, long time."

HAL HIGDON, *THE MARATHONERS*

"The eternal challenge of any marathoner—old or young, fast or slow, male or female—is to finish. To accomplish this, every runner must increase his own capacity for pain."

JOE FALLS, *THE BOSTON MARATHON*

"The marathon is not the most arduous sport, as it's commonly known, but the most perfect sport for the human organism."

EMIL ZATOPEK IN *MARATHONING* BY MANFRED STEFFNY

"Racing is where I have to face the truth about myself."

JOE HENDERSON, *JOG, RUN, RACE*

———•••••———

"As I began the final mile of the New York City Marathon . . . I was not dancing, I was not singing. Now it was a little hard to concentrate on anything other than running, as though I had gone blind."

RICHARD HARTEIS, *MARATHON: A STORY OF ENDURANCE AND FRIENDSHIP*

———•••••———

"Each runner was trying to conserve his power of concentration for use during the time when concentration would be in great demand, during the last nine miles, and trying to be at peace with himself and his surroundings. The peace helps to preserve the adrenaline."

THOMAS BARRETT AND ROBERT MORRISSEY, *MARATHON RUNNERS*

"I kept going, down Beacon street, striding forever in an endless corridor of humanity, running on protesting legs . . . As I crossed the finish line I heard a guy say, 'Number 534 is 441st.' 'It's all over,' a girl told me, reading out. 'No,' I told her, 'It's just started.'"

JOHN ROMERO, "BACK AMONG THE LEGIONS," IN *BOSTON: AMERICA'S OLDEST MARATHON*

"If you're running a marathon only to get a feel for what it's like to run in a marathon, it's senseless to line up at the starting line."

RICHARD BENYO, *MAKING THE MARATHON YOUR EVENT*

"The purpose of fueling yourself during the marathon is to avoid low blood sugar—the first indication that the Wall is looming—and to refuel your muscles with carbohydrates."

DAVE KUEHLS, *4 MONTHS TO A 4 HOUR MARATHON*

———

"I can apparently run 20 miles up on my toes and feel absolutely fine, but then my feet get tired and I turn into a flat-footed six-minute-per-mile plodder."

ANNE AUDAIN (AND JOHN L. PARKER) IN *UNCOMMON HEART*

———

"The little engine driving my soul kicked into overdrive and produced something like dream power."

RICHARD HARTEIS, *MARATHON: A STORY OF ENDURANCE AND FRIENDSHIP*

"I love racing against somebody else and proving myself stronger than him, making him suffer."

DEREK CLAYTON, WINNER OF THE 1968 MEXICO CITY MARATHON, IN *MARATHONS: THE ULTIMATE CHALLENGE* BY JOEL HOMER

"I think old age is a social disease that people think they cannot overcome. For those who really want to go for it, I hope this will be an inspiration."

PRICILLA WELCH, ON WINNING THE NEW YORK CITY MARATHON IN 1987, IN *THE NEW YORK CITY MARATHON: TWENTY-FIVE YEARS*

"My shirt read, 'I AM 50 AND GOING THE DISTANCE.' The crowd responded. 'I don't believe it.' 'Looking good, sister.'"

DOLORES E. CROSS, *BREAKING THROUGH THE WALL*

"The Marathon Begins at 20 Miles."

FRANK SHORTER IN *THE RUNNING TIMES GUIDE TO BREAKTHROUGH RUNNING*

"Taking a well-trained body through a grueling 26.2 mile race does immeasurably more for the self concept and self-esteem than years with the best psychiatrist."

GEORGE SHEEHAN IN *PERSONAL BEST*

"I wasn't certain of winning until I made the last turn about 200 yards from the finish . . . Before that I was just busting like hell, worrying like hell all the way. But this is a good thing to develop, you know: the fear. It keeps you moving."

RON HILL, 1970 BOSTON MARATHON WINNER, IN *MARATHON MYTHOLOGY*

"The idea is to clear your mind of everything and to let your body function naturally, undisturbed by thoughts."

COACH KIYOSKI NAKAMURA, ABOUT COACHING TOSHIHIKO SEKO, IN *COMPETITIVE EDGE* BY RICHARD ELLIOTT

"I race hard, because I know no other way to race than to rub against the jagged edge of exhaustion."

JOE HENDERSON, *RUN FARTHER, RUN FASTER*

"I suppose I knew it all along—that unless I ran I'd never really know what was behind the faces of the finishers."

MARK OSMUN, *THE HONOLULU MARATHON*

"I didn't know whether or not my mind was willing to put my body through it."

FRANK SHORTER, ON WINNING THE 1972 MUNICH OLYMPIC MARATHON, IN *MARATHON RUNNERS* BY THOMAS BARRETT AND ROBERT MORRISSEY

"The wall can appear at any time, for anyone. Only you can break through the wall and find what's on the other side."

DOLORES E. CROSS, *BREAKING THROUGH THE WALL*

"My whole feeling, in terms of racing, is that you have to be very bold. You sometimes have to be aggressive and gamble."

BILL ROGERS IN *MARATHONING*

"You must be fast enough. You must have endurance. So you run fast for speed and repeat it many times for endurance."

EMIL ZATOPEK

"How am I? The race is the answer, the only answer. The runner is truly a man dissatisfied with the status quo. His object is to reach goals that are continually being reset."

GEORGE SHEEHAN IN *DR. GEORGE SHEEHAN ON RUNNING*

"It became a matter of singular concentration, discipline, monomania. I had to zero in on one thing . . . I just made up my mind to work and see how good I could be. I didn't want to quit and say for the rest of my life 'Well, maybe I could have been.'"

FRANK SHORTER IN *MARATHON RUNNERS* BY THOMAS BARRETT AND ROBERT MORRISSEY

"Too many people think about 26 miles and they panic. My philosophy has always been—run one mile at a time and enjoy each mile."

IBRA MORALES, NEW YORK, NY

"Racing is the lovemaking of the runner. It's hard to pass up."

GEORGE SHEEHAN IN *HEROES AND SPARROWS*

"Moments before, we were mere mortals. Now, standing proudly in front of the mirror, checking to see that the number is straight and properly placed, we are warriors. . . . Like all great warriors, we stand ready to face the enemy. In most cases, that enemy is ourselves."

JOHN "THE PENGUIN" BINGHAM, *THE COURAGE TO START*

"Men, today we die a little."

EMIL ZATOPEK

"Work against your natural pacing instincts. Hold back when you feel like pushing in the first half-marathon. Push when you feel like slowing in the second half."

JOE HENDERSON

"If you feel bad at 10 miles, you're in trouble. If you feel bad at 20 miles, you're normal. If you don't feel bad at 26 miles, you're abnormal."

ROB DE CASTELLA IN THE QUOTABLE RUNNER

"Three hours? Three hours? I don't even like to do things that feel GOOD for three hours!"

ACTRESS GWYNETH PALTROW RESPONDING TO REPORTER TOM VOELK'S STATEMENT THAT IT WOULD TAKE HIM ROUGHLY 3 HOURS TO RUN THE NYC MARATHON

"It begins about 30 minutes from the finish line. You find yourself chastising yourself for this foolishness, and promising yourself if you just finish you will never put yourself through such self-imposed torture again. Within 30 minutes after you complete the race, you have experienced the relief and recovery. Then you forget about all the pain and begin planning for your next marathon."

TED BAUER, POWAY, CA

"We were a sickly lot by now, like refugees staggering across the border."

RICHARD HARTEIS, *MARATHON: A STORY OF ENDURANCE AND FRIENDSHIP*

———•+••———

"As a reporter writing about the running in the 100th Boston Marathon, I was asked by a race official the day after 40,000 of us completed the trek from Hopkington to Boston if there was anything I would change about the race: 'Yes,' I said. 'Cut it to 13 miles.'"

STEVE NEARMAN, *WASHINGTON TIMES*

"My physical distress at having my heart, lungs and legs work at abnormal speed and the mental difficulty of keeping my body at the task was such that the one thing I dreaded was interruption or distraction of any kind. Any word or deed aimed to get my attention would be like throwing a monkey wrench into a finely geared piece of machinery."

CLARENCE DEMAR, REFLECTIONS ON THE 1936 BOSTON MARATHON, *MARATHON: THE CLARENCE DEMAR STORY*

"The marathon's about being in contention over the last 10K. That's when it's about what you have in your core. You have run all the strength, all the superficial fitness out of yourself, and it really comes down to what's left inside you. To be able to draw deep and pull something out of yourself is one of the most tremendous things about the marathon."

ROB DE CASTELLA IN *THE QUOTABLE RUNNER*

"The marathon is like a bullfight. There are two ways to kill a bull, for instance. There is the easy way, for one. But all the great matadors end up either dead or mauled because for them killing the bull is not nearly as important as how they kill the bull. They always approach the bull as the greatest risk to themselves, and I admire that. In the marathon, likewise, there are two ways to win. There's the easy way if all you care about is winning. You hang back and risk nothing. Then kick and try to nip the leaders at the end. Or you can push, challenge the others, make it an exciting race, risking everything. Maybe you lose, for as for me, I'd rather run a gutsy race, pushing all the way and lose, than run a conservative, easy race only for a win."

ALBERTO SALAZAR IN *THE QUOTABLE RUNNER*

"It's two races: a 20 and a 6. The whole thing is the six miler. That's when focus, form and will come into play. I have some kind of mantra I repeat endlessly in the final phase. This year it was 'Form follows function.' Last year it was 'Stay in the box,' meaning imagine myself contained in a small box, keep the arms and legs and even the will inside the box. It changes the emphasis from goal to process."

LENNARD DAVIS, BRONX, NY

———•••••———

"Right in the snapping teeth of death, I dance and laugh. Knowing in a vague yet entirely wonderful way that this is the way I give honor and glory to God."

THADDEUS KOSTRUBALA, *THE JOY OF RUNNING*

"Run even splits! Very few runners have run fast on this course without running even splits. Unless your name is Joan Benoit, you can't throw out the rule book: Joan went through 10 miles in 51:38 when she set the record back in '83 . . . but that's Joanie."

BOB SEVENE, COACH, "HOW TO RUN THE BOSTON MARATHON COURSE," IN *THE QUOTABLE RUNNER*

———

"I would say when participating in any warmup, especially one before the marathon, do not attempt to do any stretching or movement that you haven't done on a regular basis. If they're jogging in place, doing breathing exercises, fine. But I think the most important thing for people to do before the race is hydrate, relax, and get to the starting line as calmly as possible."

STU MITTLEMAN IN *THE ESSENTIAL MARATHONER*

"Once underway, your most important task is to find the right pace and to stick to it. Starting too fast is a common mistake. At the beginning you should feel as if you're going a bit too slowly. If your pace is too quick, fatigue will force you to slow down later. The body is parsimonious with its energy supply; there's only so much available."

JAMES FIXX, *THE COMPLETE BOOK OF RUNNING*

"'What does a fellow think about when he's running one of those long grinds?' How many times have I been asked that! Whatever I may think myself may not apply to others, but some of the general things that go through a marathoner's mind will be the same . . . all agree to a tenseness and fear and uncertainty about something."

CLARENCE DEMAR, *MARATHON: THE CLARENCE DEMAR STORY*

"Horray for me! I scaled Mount Everest, pitched a no-hitter in the World Series and killed the meanest bull in Madrid. That is what it felt like when I won the 1975 Boston Marathon in 4 hours 16 minutes. Will Rogers thinks he won the Marathon in 2 hours 9 minutes and 55 seconds, but he was wrong. Or, to be more accurate, he was running a different race."

RICHARD J. ISRAEL, *NEW YORK TIMES* EDITORIAL (1975)

"Now I wish I had crawled the rest of the way on my hands and knees. It is difficult to live with the fact you've quit. It's like having a prison record."

HAL HIGDON IN *THE BOSTON MARATHON* BY JOE FALLS

"After holding back for over an hour of running, I let my anxiety get the better of me at the halfway point. I felt like I was now far enough along that I could finally open up and run. My legs still felt good so I was tricked into running faster for miles 13, 14 and 15, but when I reached 18 the tables had turned . . . my pace slowed a bit after 23 and my only thoughts were to get to the finish."

BRIAN CLAS, NEW YORK, NY, WINNER OF THE 2000 PHILADELPHIA MARATHON

"The object of the game in racing is to find the pace that you can just hold, that you think is going to kill you but that doesn't—quite. This is a species of self-torture that makes nonexercisers mumble the word 'sick,' but I don't think it is."

JOHN JEROME, *THE ELEMENTS OF EFFORT*

"Running a successful marathon is an exercise is holding back. Ideally, the hard work shouldn't begin until 20 miles. Then your training and willpower will get you to the finish. During the race remain calm and focused. Note your splits, and take encouragement from a steady pace early on, even if others are passing you."

GORDAN BAKOULIS BLOCH IN *RUNNER'S WORLD COMPLETE BOOK OF RUNNING*

"Some people say the marathon does not begin until 20 miles. That's when you hit the wall. The real truth is that the first few miles are the most important ones of the race. People who make mistakes in the early miles by going out too hard or by not taking enough water are the ones who aren't going to win the race, or, perhaps, even finish it."

BILL ROGERS IN *RUNNING WITH THE LEGENDS*

"The wall looms before you at just about mile 20, sometimes before and sometimes after. The body, mind, and spirit come to what feels like a running in place, a great yawning pause, a frustrating inertia . . ."

DOLORES E. CROSS, *BREAKING THROUGH THE WALL*

"Somewhere around mile twenty, it hit me. Instead of a wall, I found the truth. . . . I looked at those who, like me, were running in measured strides. I saw the look of determination in their faces. I saw the roll of twenty miles of fighting against an uncooperative body, I saw the strain of overcoming years of failure. I saw it in them, and they saw it in me."

JOHN "THE PENGUIN" BINGHAM, *THE COURAGE TO START*

"My opinion is that the 'wall' is more mental than physical. As long as you've prepared well in your training and been smart in the early stages, you should be fine. Don't let your mind seek out something negative by expecting to 'hit the wall' once you hit 20 miles."

BRIAN CLAS, NEW YORK, NY, WINNER OF THE 2000 PHILADELPHIA MARATHON

"Racing is like building a house. The first ninety percent of the race takes ninety percent of your resources. The remaining ten percent of the race takes another ninety percent of your resources."

JOHN JEROME, *THE ELEMENTS OF EFFORT*

"Running the marathon gave me an inner strength that changed my life. I think that's what happens to a lot of women who complete a marathon. Whether it's fast or slow, whether you walk some of it or not, just finishing can have a profound affect on your confidence and self-esteem."

HENLEY GIBBLE IN *THE ESSENTIAL RUNNER*

———————

"It was suddenly all worth it. I had won. I had refused to accept a bad back, the middle-aged paunch of a sedentary rabbi, even my mortality, and had triumphed over them."

RICHARD J. ISRAEL, *NEW YORK TIMES* EDITORIAL (1975)

"I'm starting to cry. I'm remembering those years I struggled with my weight, those times when I saw my reflection in a store window and didn't know who that fat person was, years when it was a big accomplishment for me to exercise at two dots on the StairMaster. And now I'm finishing a 26-mile race. Damn! This is better than winning an Emmy!"

OPRAH WINFREY IN *THE ESSENTIAL MARATHONER*

"The challenge of a significant physical journey on foot unleashes some primitive connections to our identity as human beings."

JEFF GALLOWAY, *MARATHON*

"A marathon doesn't finish at the finish line. Exciting and memorable as it is, it leaves behind physical damage, both obvious and subtle, that takes weeks to clear. Recover well."

JOE HENDERSON

"At some level, running a marathon is easy. It's getting yourself prepared, that's where all the effort is. And a large part of that effort is mental."

AMBY BURFOOT IN *THE ESSENTIAL MARATHONER*

"In order to be successful in the marathon, you have to know exactly what you want out of it."

BILL ROGERS IN *MARATHONING*

"The marathon is a race of attrition. There are very, very few marathoners—even among the top level—who can go out fast and hold it for the entire race. Try to exercise self-control. That's how you run a good marathon: by running the first half slower than the second."

MIKE KEOHANE IN *THE ESSENTIAL MARATHONER*

"By this time, none of us was running a race. We were trying to help one another survive an ordeal. There was no loneliness among the long distance runners."

RICHARD J. ISRAEL, *NEW YORK TIMES* EDITORIAL (1975)

"Every marathon becomes a theater for heroic acts."

GEORGE SHEEHAN IN *BOSTON: A CENTURY OF RUNNING*

"The race, the marathon, is a renewal of belief in one's self and the ultimate expression of confidence that you have created the foundation that enables you to go the distance."

DOLORES E. CROSS, *BREAKING THROUGH THE WALL*

"Boston is not a race. It's a state of mind created by a knowledgeable and enthusiastic crowd that doesn't merely watch, it actively participates in the race. Those who cheered me had as much to do with my finish as I did."

KEVIN DONAHUE IN *BOSTON: A CENTURY OF RUNNING*

"In the finishing chutes we all hugged each other. I hugged the man in front of me and the one behind me."

MARK OSMUN, *THE HONOLULU MARATHON*

"I tell myself to relax each part of the body: neck, shoulders, arms. Then I repeat some words like 'steady, push' to keep up the pace and confidence."

GRETE WAITZ IN *THE ESSENTIAL MARATHONER*

"Running the marathon is not only the most dramatic way I know to fight my illness. It is also my message to the many other sufferers of this disease who have sought from me a bit of advice or inspiration. The question is not why I'm doing it. The question is, 'Why aren't you doing it, too?'"

FRED LEBOW, ON RUNNING AND HIS BATTLE WITH CANCER, IN *THE NEW YORK CITY MARATHON: TWENTY-FIVE YEARS*

"Treat the marathon as your graduation exercise. In those few hours, celebrate the good work that made this day possible. It's your reward for all the effort put in over the last few months."

JOE HENDERSON, *MARATHON TRAINING*

"There's an old adage that for every second too fast per mile in the first half of the race, you'll run at least 2 seconds slower at the end."

JEFF GALLOWAY, *GALLOWAY'S BOOK ON RUNNING*

"Everyone wins the marathon. We all have the same feeling at the start—nervous, anxious, excited. It is a broader, richer, and—even with twenty-seven thousand people—more intimate experience than I found when I was racing in track. New York is the marathon that all the biggest stars want to win, but it has also been the stage for an array of human stories more vast than any other sporting event."

GRETE WAITZ IN *THE NEW YORK CITY MARATHON: TWENTY-FIVE YEARS*

———

"Even the latest finishers aren't back-of-the-packers. They're the back of the front, still among the elite one-tenth of one percent of Americans who can and does finish the marathon."

JOE HENDERSON

"Finally I came upon another lone spectator, and I asked him, 'How much farther?' 'Just a couple of miles,' he replied. I just lost it. I screamed, 'That's what you told me way back there, you liar.' Of course he must have thought I was a total lunatic, because he hadn't told me any such thing—the other guy had! That's how disoriented I was."

CLIFF HELD IN *HOW TO TRAIN FOR AND RUN YOUR BEST MARATHON*

⸻

"Sooner or later, in every marathon, I begin to laugh. There's a foolishness about marathons that is obvious to everyone except those who attempt to run them. Except perhaps for the truly gifted athletes, one must have a sense of humor about the act of running 26.2 miles for no particular reason."

JOHN "THE PENGUIN" BINGHAM, *THE COURAGE TO START*

"The marathon is about taking on the realities of a given day, a given body, and given conditions, and simply doing the best with them that one possibly can, then watching to see what unfolds."

GORDON BAKOULIS BLOCH, *HOW TO TRAIN FOR AND RUN YOUR BEST MARATHON*

"No weaklings will be permitted to start in the marathon tomorrow."

BOSTON HERALD, APRIL 18, 1900, IN *THE BOSTON MARATHON* BY TOM DERDERIAN

"How'd I do it? . . . I ran with patience."

JOHN A. KELLY, ON WINNING THE 1945 BOSTON MARATHON, IN *BOSTON MARATHON* BY TOM DERDERIAN

"Run the first half as a 'pacer.' Ignore the people around you who dash away from the starting line; keep your head as they lose theirs. Run like a scientist, with coolness, wisdom and restraint."

JOE HENDERSON, *RUN FARTHER, RUN FASTER*

"Holding back is a wise strategy in any marathon."

BILL ROGERS IN *MARATHONING*

"In the marathon, nothing is over until the finish."

GRETE WAITZ IN *THE NEW YORK CITY MARATHON: TWENTY-FIVE YEARS*

"Hold yourself back, you should have a conscious feeling in the first half of the race that you could be running a lot faster."

GORDON BAKOULIS BLOCH, *HOW TO TRAIN FOR AND RUN YOUR BEST MARATHON*

"I always feel that it is a good strategy to use the early part of the race to position yourself for a strong finish, but with the marathon you can feel confident and controlled at one point only to feel fatigued and struggling a few miles later."

BRIAN CLAS, NEW YORK, NY, WINNER OF THE 2000 PHILADELPHIA MARATHON

"In the last six miles, think of how many times you've run a 10-K before. Focus on your achievements. You've trained hard. You deserve your best. You're already through. Tell yourself how tough you are."

DAVID COWEIN IN *MARATHON: THE ULTIMATE TRAINING GUIDE*

"The 26.2-mile distance tends to make all runners prudent, cautious and respectful. 'Anyone,' said the great Percy Cerutty, 'can run twenty miles, but only a few can run the marathon.' The extra six miles changes the game from penny ante to table stakes. Your entire physical bankroll can dissolve in a matter of minutes."

GEORGE SHEEHAN, *RUNNING AND BEING*

"How dull it is to pause, to make an end, to rush unburnished, not to shine in use."

ALFRED LORD TENNYSON, "ULYSSES"

Reflections

"The marathon is my only girlfriend. I give her every-thing I have."

TOSHIHIKO SEKO

Something about the movement of my feet against the pavement or grass gets my mind rolling. I ruminate on the progression of my life and the meaning of love.

The run is over. Nothing is solved, but somehow I feel better. The joy of moving has made me pure again, returned me to the primitive, peeled away the layers that keep me from myself. I face my own inadequacies with renewed vigor.

Sometimes I think that everyone who trains for a marathon is rehearsing to remake a life too often trapped in what William Wordsworth refers to as the "getting and spending" of daily existence.

The quotes collected in this chapter represent some of the finest reflective thinking about distance running. They are proof that those who run develop a unique relationship to themselves and to the world. Marathoners are both insiders and outsiders, able to see more clearly because of our difference from others, and also because of our closeness to that which is vital in life—such moments as when we traverse a field while the sun is painting the horizon purple and yellow and orange.

"Where have all the heroes gone?" asks George Sheehan. "They've gone with the simplicities and the pieties and the easy answers of another era. Our lack of heroes is an indication of the maturity of our age. A realization that every man has come into his own and has the capability of making a success out of his life. But also that this success rests with having the courage and endurance and, above all, the will to become the person you are, however peculiar that may be. Then you will be able to say, 'I have found my hero and he is me.'"

Similarly, *Love Story* writer Erich Segal ruminates: "In this mechanized society of ours, marathoners want to assert their individuality more than ever. Call it humanism, call it health, call it folly. Some are Lancelots, most are Don Quixotes. All are noble."

Or Thaddeus Kostrubala: "As I run, I recall previous runs, previous pain, earlier marathons. Little bits and pieces come into me again. I hope I have exhumed the want. Perhaps not. Dying may be something like this. I hope it is. I would like to die like Zorba, screaming and fighting to live. It's my dedication to life. . . . I want to be me forever."

Or Mark Hanson: "To run is to live. Everything else is just waiting." Or, finally, Joe Henderson: "All my troubles come from running. Then I use running to go out and get rid of them."

"You have to forget your last marathon before you run another. Your mind knows what's coming."

FRANK SHORTER TO KENNY MOORE IN *SPORTS ILLUSTRATED*

———

"As we become increasingly involved in technology, science, and business, we should not lose that instinct, that feeling for the earth. Running is a very beautiful way to bring out those healthy feelings."

BILL ROGERS IN *MARATHON RUNNERS*

———

"In our ever-more-mechanized, programmed society, marathoners want to assert their independence and affirm their individuality . . . call it humanism, call it health, call it folly. Some are Lancelots, most are Don Quixotes. All are noble. Whatever it is, our ailing world could use a lot more of it."

ERICH SEGAL IN *THE BOSTON MARATHON* BY JOE FALLS

"There isn't much freedom in our lives any more. Running gives you freedom. When you run, you can go at your own speed. You can go where you want to go and think your own thoughts. Nobody has any claim on you."

NINA KUSCSIK, WINNER OF THE 1972 WOMEN'S DIVISION OF
THE BOSTON MARATHON, IN *THE COMPLETE BOOK OF RUNNING*

———

"I think you need to enjoy life. God gives you one chance to do it. We might as well take it as far as we can, and running a marathon is doing just that."

JOSH VANCE, FIRST LIEUTENANT OF THE MARINES, AFTER
COMPLETING THE LOS ANGELES MARATHON, MARCH 2001

"There is a high burnout rate among time goal marathoners ... If the satisfaction is derived solely on the clock at the finish, most of the joys of running slip by, underappreciated.

JEFF GALLOWAY, *MARATHON*

"This obsession with running is really an obsession with the potential for more and more life."

GEORGE SHEEHAN, *DR. GEORGE SHEEHAN ON RUNNING*

"There is a marathon lifestyle. It is called sacrifice. I would like to exemplify it more than I do."

PHIL CURATILO IN *THE MARATHON: WHAT IT TAKES TO GO THE DISTANCE* BY MARK BLOOM

"Marathoning provides you with a unique challenge. It pushes your body to its limits, but above all, it challenges you to come to terms with yourself, your fears and your strengths. Through the process you gain a deeper knowledge of yourself, if you are prepared to look."

GARY ELLIOTT, ALLISON ROE'S COACH AND CO-AUTHOR OF *EVERY RUNNER'S COMPANION*

———————

"I will win without shoes. I will make some history for Africa."

ABEBE BIKILA, TWO-TIME WINNER OF THE OLYMPIC MARATHON, ON HIS DECISION TO RUN BAREFOOT. "BIKILA'S TRIUMPH, TRAGEDY" BY DAVE PROKOP, IN *THE COMPLETE MARATHONER*

"Do most of us want life on the same calm level as a geometrical problem? Certainly we want our pleasures more varied with both mountains and valleys of emotional joy, and marathoning furnishes just that."

CLARENCE DEMAR, *MARATHON: THE CLARENCE DEMAR STORY*

———•——

"As I run, I recall previous runs, previous pain, earlier marathons. Little bits and pieces come into me again. I hope I have exhumed the want. Perhaps not. Dying may be something like this. I hope it is. I would like to die like Zorba, screaming and fighting to live. It's my dedication to life. To all life. Somehow I am too Western. I like the word 'occidental.' I hate the word 'amorphous.' I want to be me, forever."

THADDEUS KOSTRUBALA, *THE JOY OF RUNNING*

"We are different, in essence, from other men. If you want to win something, run 100 meters. If you want to experience something, run a marathon."

EMIL ZATOPEK IN *THE QUOTABLE RUNNER*

"The difference between the mile and the marathon is the difference between burning your fingers with a match and being slowly roasted over hot coals."

HAL HIGDON IN *THE COMPLETE BOOK OF RUNNING*

"There are some people who run for pleasure, to reduce tension, to stay healthy. But this marathoning is something different . . . What I do is bordering on the exhibitionist . . . one word will sum it up. Ego. Just plain ego."

WALTER STACK IN *MARATHON RUNNERS*

"The marathon is a celebration of the human spirit. You reaffirm to yourself your willingness to compete, and that helps you in everyday challenges that you take on. It gives you that extra confidence."

DARREN CARPIZO, AFTER COMPLETING THE LOS ANGELES MARATHON, MARCH 2001

"Running is like getting back to the core. It is like being wild again. I'm running because a lot of my friends encouraged me to share feelings of joy I get while I'm running. It is hard to explain. The other runners understand."

BOBBI GIBB, FIRST WOMAN TO RUN THE BOSTON MARATHON, IN *BOSTON MARATHON* BY TOM DERDERIAN

"I have been asked everywhere I go: Why do people run the marathon? Sure, there is a sense of status we gain among our peers. But I think the real reasons are personal. I think it is because we need to test our physical, emotional, or creative abilities. After all, in practical life we cannot all 'give it our all.' . . . the marathon gives us a stage. In this case, it's the road, where we can perform and be proud, while millions of people applaud. It's like being on Broadway and getting a standing ovation!"

GEORGE SHEEHAN IN *THE NEW YORK ROAD RUNNERS CLUB COMPLETE BOOK OF RUNNING AND FITNESS*

"It's an unvicious cycle; when I am happy I am running well and when I am running well I am happy. . . . It is the Platonic idea of knowing thyself. Running is getting to know yourself to an extreme degree."

IAN THOMPSON IN *THE MARATHON: WHAT IT TAKES TO GO THE DISTANCE* BY MARK BLOOM

"The marathon has around it a halo of deep, symbolic meaning."

EMIL ZATOPEK IN *MARATHONING* BY MANFRED STEFFNY

"In the struggling faces of the runners is written a dimension of human experience that cost me dearly, but, at least on marathon day, seems worth the price."

JEROME GROOPMAN IN THE *NEW YORK TIMES*

"Within running, the marathon has come to hold a very special place . . . it is a race with a name, not a number like the 100-yard dash or the 10,000 meters—a name that, like 'the mile,' reinforces its identity."

MARK BLOOM, *THE MARATHON: WHAT IT TAKES TO GO THE DISTANCE*

"Completing a marathon is a feeling that you can't buy. You have to earn it. The experience is what you make of it. The camaraderie is awesome."

DAN MORIHIKO, AFTER COMPLETING THE LOS ANGELES MARATHON, MARCH 2001

"We run, not because we think it is doing us good, but because we enjoy it and cannot help ourselves. It also does us good because it helps us to do other things better. It gives a man or woman the chance to bring out power that might otherwise remain locked away inside. The urge to struggle lies latent in everyone."

ROGER BANNISTER, *THE FOUR MINUTE MILE*

"I did it because I am turning 50 soon. I'd like to see whether I can do it in the next 50 years."

LARRY SILVERSTEIN, AFTER COMPLETING THE LOS ANGELES MARATHON, MARCH 2001

"Feel the flow of your dance and know you are not running for some future reward—the reward is now!"

FRED ROHE, *THE ZEN OF RUNNING*

"The question is not why I run this way, but why so many others cannot."

LASSE VIREN, "TRAINING TO PEAK," IN *MAKE YOUR OWN TIME* BY RON DAVIS

"The challenge in running is not to aim at doing the things no one else has done, but to keep doing things anyone could do—but most never will."

JOE HENDERSON IN *THE COMPLETE BOOK OF RUNNING*

"Maybe it's time to admit that running 26.22 miles is as irrational and illogical as batting a fuzzy ball back and forth across a net, chasing a little white ball around a golf course, or committing assault and battery between two sets of goal posts. None of these games serves any great purpose, none has any great importance to the survival of mankind, but they all have great meaning to the people involved. That's all we should ask of our play."

JOE HENDERSON, "MEANING OF THE MARATHON," IN
THE COMPLETE MARATHONER

"Long-distance running is the new sublimation, the ultimate in deferred gratification. . . . For his own protection, the marathoner must develop an infinite capacity to endure boredom."

BOSTON GLOBE EDITORIAL, 1979, IN *BOSTON: AMERICA'S OLDEST MARATHON*

"Running is essentially private and, if you like, selfish, and all the more valuable for being so."

ROGER ROBINSON, *HEROES AND SPARROWS: A CELEBRATION OF RUNNING*

———————

"I just gave myself a 70th birthday present! It's a solitary sport but what I like is that I can set my own agenda for it as far as pace and time. This year I talked my 39-year-old into doing it with me, which was great."

BILL STEINAUER, AFTER COMPLETING THE LOS ANGELES MARATHON, MARCH 2001

———————

"The marathoner is the runner who continually searches for the perfect run and, in the process, is more than satisfied with the physical and psychological benefits the marathon lifestyle bestows during the process of the quest."

RICHARD BENYO, *MAKING THE MARATHON YOUR EVENT*

"The genuine marathoner is a rare breed indeed: half athlete and half poet; part rock-bottom pragmatist and part sky-high idealist; completely, even defiantly individual and yet irrevocably joined to a select group almost tribal in its shared rituals and aspirations."

JOEL HOMER, *MARATHONS: THE ULTIMATE CHALLENGE*

"Racing is a voluntary act of self-abuse. Before you decide to do it, you must be very sure this is what you want."

JOE HENDERSON, *JOG, RUN, RACE*

"I don't think you can become an outstanding runner unless you get a certain amount of enjoyment out of the suffering. You have to enjoy absorbing it, controlling it and—ultimately—overcoming it."

DEREK CLAYTON IN *THE MASTERS OF THE MARATHON*

"I am too tired, even to be happy."

GELINDO BORDIN, ITALY, AFTER WINNING THE OLYMPIC MARATHON
IN SEOUL, IN *THE QUOTABLE RUNNER*

"Winners say what they want to happen. Losers say what they feel will happen."

DR. LINDA BUNKER IN *JOAN SAMUELSON'S RUNNING FOR WOMEN*

"Humans were made to run."

ALBERTO SALAZAR, *ALBERTO SALAZAR'S GUIDE TO RUNNING*

"A runner's two worst enemies on the road are dogs and people."

DAVE KUEHLS, *4 MONTHS TO A 4 HOUR MARATHON*

"Only dogs and wolves are as well built for long-distance running as humans."

ALBERTO SALAZAR, *ALBERTO SALAZAR'S GUIDE TO RUNNING*

———

"I feel that slow long-distance running is not a sport at all. It is an activity that resonates with our biological heritage. And, in so resonating, we may be able to penetrate the confines of our circumstance and establish a better harmony with ourselves and our world."

THADDEUS KOSTRUBALA, *THE JOY OF RUNNING*

"There are few experiences in life in which my physical and psychological abilities are as sharply defined as they are during marathon training and racing . . . The training and racing experiences have shown me sides of myself that I never knew existed. I've found perseverance, an ability to focus, stubbornness, compulsiveness, bravery, organization, a sense of humor, and a capacity for unbridled joy."

GORDON BAKOULIS BLOCH, *HOW TO TRAIN FOR AND RUN YOUR BEST MARATHON*

———•••••———

"To do any creative act, you must have an experience. Any race is such an experience, but the marathon is that experience raised to the nth degree. It fills the conscious and unconscious with sights and sounds, feelings and emotions, trials and accomplishments. And in the end, we know creation."

GEORGE SHEEHAN IN *PERSONAL BEST*

"Unless you can perceive yourself as someone who is going to be a good runner, you're never going to be one."

GARY ELLIOTT AND ALLISON ROE, *EVERY RUNNER'S COMPANION*

———

"The only real failure is the failure to try."

JOAN BENOIT, *RUNNING TIDE*

———

"At least 99 percent of running is just showing up, getting out there and putting one foot in front of the other."

JOHN HANC, *THE ESSENTIAL RUNNER*

"Anyone can run 20 miles. But few can run a marathon."

PERCY CERUTTY, AUSTRALIAN COACH, IN *APRIL IN THE HILLS* BY GEORGE SHEEHAN

———◦•❖•◦———

"The seed of an idea grows into a goal, and from the goal sprouts a plan. The plan blossoms into training and finally matures as racing fitness."

JOE HENDERSON, *THE COMPLETE MARATHONER*

———◦•❖•◦———

"We have been told time and again we were born to success, but a truly run marathon convinces us of that truth."

GEORGE SHEEHAN IN *PERSONAL BEST*

"I somehow sensed that the marathon sprang from greatness to inspire greatness."

DOROTHY DESLONGCHAMPS IN *BOSTON* BY HAL HIGDON

"Life is a desperate struggle to succeed in being in fact that which we are in design."

JOSÉ ORTEGA Y GASSET

"I never felt as bad as I did over those last two miles. It was like running with a hangover. Like having gone out and partied yourself to death and trying to get up the next morning."

GEOFF SMITH, RUNNER-UP TO THE 1983 NYC MARATHON, IN *THE QUOTABLE RUNNER*

"He runs like a man who has just been stabbed in the heart."

EUROPEAN COACH ON EMIL ZATOPEK

"A runner is a miser, spending the pennies of his energy with great stinginess, constantly wanting to know how much he has spent and how much longer he will be expected to pay. He wants to be broke at precisely the moment he no longer needs his coin."

JOHN L. PARKER, *ONCE A RUNNER*

"The trick is to stop seeing yourself as trapped inside a limited body capable only of performance that is only controlled by that body, but rather know that your true nature lives as perfection, limitless across time and space."

RICHARD BACH, *JONATHON LIVINGSTON SEAGULL*

"There are times when the thought of running a marathon quite frightens me."

> IAN THOMPSON, FORMER MARATHON WORLD RECORD HOLDER, IN *THE COMPLETE MARATHONER*

"We have these fear barriers . . . back off points. And a lot of them are unfounded. We haven't even touched on what we're capable of yet. And we won't—not until we can break the chains that have our minds tied to our bodies."

> GARY ELLIOTT, ALLISON ROE'S COACH AND CO-AUTHOR OF *EVERY RUNNER'S COMPANION*

"The power to achieve, to regulate one's life with regard to self-indulgence, or abstinence, comes from within. Any superimposed authority over things like this shows as much sense as commanding the sun and moon stand still."

> CLARENCE DEMAR, *MARATHON: THE CLARENCE DEMAR STORY*

"To be able to run to perfection, you must begin by knowing you've been there already."

RICHARD BACH IN *EVERY RUNNER'S COMPANION* BY ALLISON ROE AND GARY ELLIOTT

"Being an athlete is a state of mind which is not bound by age, performance or place in the running pack."

JEFF GALLOWAY, *GALLOWAY'S BOOK ON RUNNING*

"Be aware to challenge your fear of learning."

RICHARD BACH, *JONATHAN LIVINGSTON SEAGULL*

"The marathon lifestyle promotes doing rather than watching . . . by adopting the marathon lifestyle you can confront your own lions, be your own hero, fight your own battles, challenge yourself."

RICHARD BENYO, *MAKING THE MARATHON YOUR EVENT*

"To give anything less than your best is to sacrifice the Gift."

STEVE PREFONTAINE, IN *PRE* BY TOM JORDAN

"None of us gets to and through the marathon alone. Dedicate your marathon to someone who runs alongside you in spirit on the big day."

JOE HENDERSON

"Some days you eat the mountain, some days the mountain eats you."

KELLY SMITH, LEAGUE CITY, TEXAS

"Marathoners don't get older. We simply change age groups."

GASPER "GABE" ABENE, CHALMETTE, LA

"Running takes me back to square one. It gives me a basic measure of accomplishment from which all other challenges take relevance."

BRIAN MCLLRATH, DANBURY, CT

"Pain is a higher level of pleasure."

K-G NYSTROM

"When asked how people get hooked on running multiple marathons, I often suggest that it's not unlike the reason a woman may want to give birth to multiple children. . . . After 18 weeks of a mentally and physically demanding training schedule (the pregnancy), one looks forward to race day with great anticipation. When the due date arrives, there's excitement, anxiety, fear, etc. For the hours of labor during the race, one can experience shots of adrenalin combined with unspeakable pain. After crossing the finish line, there's great joy combined with the feeling that you'll never put yourself through that again."

LEO BOTTARY, ATLANTIC BEACH, FL

"No marathon is easy. It's supposed to be hard. If it weren't, then everyone would do it."

JOE HENDERSON

"The marathon—pain is certain; suffering is optional."

JOE HOWARD, BONAIRE, GA

"I was unable to walk for a whole week after that, so much did the race take out of me. But it was the most pleasant exhaustion I have ever known."

EMIL ZATOPEK'S DESCRIPTION OF THE OLYMPIC MARATHON WIN IN HELSINKI

"For a week after your marathon, do nothing."

HAL HIGDON, *MARATHON: THE ULTIMATE TRAINING GUIDE*

"Running defines me. It is a euphoric feeling I look forward to every day. It keeps me connected to life. And every November I get to witness the outpouring of compassion and spirit that this city gives to the thousands of runners who tackle our marathon."

ALLAN STEINFELD, RACE DIRECTOR, NYC MARATHON,
IN *FIRST MARATHONS*

"The marathon will test your mind as well as your legs. No matter how good your conditioning, no doubt about it, you need an extra measure of confidence for the marathon."

JOAN BENOIT SAMUELSON, *RUNNING FOR WOMEN*

"In track races, you are against one another. In the marathon, it's the event, the distance, you have to beat."

IAN THOMPSON, FORMER MARATHON WORLD RECORD HOLDER,
IN *THE COMPLETE MARATHONER*

"Marathoning is like cutting yourself unexpectedly. You dip into the pain so gradually that the damage is done before you are aware of it. Unfortunately, when awareness comes, it is excruciating."

JOHN FARRINGTON, AUSTRALIAN RUNNER,
IN *THE QUOTABLE RUNNER*

"Running tells us the good news about ourselves!"

GEORGE SHEEHAN IN *HEROES AND SPARROWS: A CELEBRATION OF RUNNING*

"The way we perform is the result of the way we see ourselves. To alter our performance we need to alter or change ourselves and it is that changing that's difficult."

GARY ELLIOTT, ALLISON ROE'S COACH AND CO-AUTHOR OF *EVERY RUNNER'S COMPANION*

"I feel about marathons the way my parents taught me to feel about the ocean: it is a mighty thing and very beautiful, but don't underestimate its capacity to hurt you."

JOAN BENOIT, *RUNNING TIDE*

"Run because you're angry. Run because you've been duped and disenfranchised from a meaningful life. Perhaps you bought the sales slogan from the culture that if you work hard and achieve, get good grades, diplomas, money or whatever, you will be happy. If you are, that's fine. Then run from fear of losing all the nice things you've got."

THADDEUS KOSTRUBALA, *THE JOY OF RUNNING*

"Don't overdo it.
Underdo it.
You aren't running because
You're trying to get somewhere."

FRED ROHE, *THE ZEN OF RUNNING*

"The perfect marathon is like the perfect wave, and every marathoner keeps looking for it."

GEORGE SHEEHAN, *DR. GEORGE SHEEHAN ON RUNNING*

"If you can do a marathon, you can do anything. It's the great test of will and endurance."

LENNARD DAVIS, BRONX, NY

"My aim in life is not to run but to awaken. CON-SCIOUSNESS requires SEEING, begins with opening to what you are."

FRED ROHE, *THE ZEN OF RUNNING*

———

"I never set out to run 250 marathons. I ran them one race at a time, just as I'd race a marathon—one mile at a time. Years later, I have the privilege of looking back on a body of work spanning 3 continents and 36 states; and I still look forward to my next marathon."

PAUL FETSCHER, WARREN STREET SOCIAL AND ATHLETIC CLUB

———

"During the winter, you head out into the darkness for a run. When spring comes, and the first crocus pokes up its head . . . you know it was worthwhile."

NINA KUSCSIK, FIRST WOMAN'S WINNER OF THE BOSTON MARATHON

"A number of years ago, I placed second in a marathon. The local newspaper reporter had seen me talk the winner into entering the race. Didn't I feel foolish? I could have won it! I reflected a moment. No! I'd rather get second in 2:29 than win it in 2:31."

PAUL FETSCHER, WARREN STREET SOCIAL AND ATHLETIC CLUB

"What's this race prove? So you prove you can run a long time, so what? If you're running to keep in shape, run two miles maybe. Okay. But this! Twenty-six miles! You gotta be a nut."

RED AUERBACH, FORMER BOSTON CELTICS COACH, IN *THE BOSTON MARATHON* BY JOE FALLS

"It's hard to understand. All I know is you've got to run. Run without knowing why through fields and woods. And the winning posts no end, even though balmy clouds might be cheering you . . . that's what the loneliness of the long-distance runner feels like."

ALAN SILLITOE, FROM HIS SCREENPLAY FOR THE CLASSIC MOVIE *THE LONELINESS OF THE LONG-DISTANCE RUNNER* (PRODUCED AND DIRECTED BY TONY RICHARDSON)

"Running feels good, like a love affair. It's like a relationship—you get out of it what you put into it."

MICHAEL DOUGLAS, IN THE MOVIE *RUNNING*

"You're going to have to make a choice between your running and your marriage."

"That," her husband replied, putting on his running shoes, "is a very easy choice."

JAMES FIXX, *THE COMPLETE BOOK OF RUNNING*

———

"Psychologists have long since quit wondering about these [marathon] boys. There are certain problems of human behavior that defy rational analysis."

BILL CUNNINGHAM, *BOSTON POST*, 1932, IN *BOSTON MARATHON* BY TOM DERDERIAN

———

"I was never a graceful runner, but then, I never have thought an athletic event should be a beauty show."

CLARENCE DEMAR, *MARATHON: THE CLARENCE DEMAR STORY*

"There has been an outbreak of what I would call the Pheidippides Complex, a psychic condition based on the myth that the first marathon runner actually dropped dead when he finished. . . . to run 26 miles—officially— is to cheat death, out-Pheidippides Pheidippides."

ERICH SEGAL IN *THE MASTERS OF THE MARATHON* BY RICHARD BENYO

"Running has improved their sex lives, made them stop smoking, cured hangovers, jet lag, ulcers, constipation, alcoholism, depression, and insomnia, and prevented the common cold."

MARILYN WELLEMEYER, *ADDICTED TO PERPETUAL MOTION,* IN *FORTUNE,* 1977

"I think it's time to change the rules. They are archaic. Women can run, and they can still be women and look like women."

KATHRINE SWITZER, *NEW YORK TIMES,* APRIL 1967

"The Boston Marathon has had more to do with liberating and promoting women's marathoning than any other race in the world."

JOE HENDERSON IN *THE QUOTABLE RUNNER*

"The American marathon footrace has evolved into a cultural performance, a chance for people to tell a story about themselves . . . that story is about community."

PAMELA COOPER, *THE AMERICAN MARATHON*

"Fitness can't be stored. It must be earned over and over, indefinitely. If a man runs for twenty years and stops completely, it is just a matter of time until he is in the same physical condition as the fellow who has never done anything."

TED CORBITT IN *THE BOSTON MARATHON* BY JOE FALLS

———◦•◦———

"The hill loomed large and his legs screamed for oxygen. He tucked his chin and thought about nothing at all, except staying smooth, light, rhythmic and relaxed. For soon his mind would wrestle the familiar demons that come with every 26.2. He concentrated."

CRICKET BATZ, WOMEN'S RUNNING COACH, UNIVERSITY OF PENNSYLVANIA

"The marathon epitomizes the mentality of a distance runner. It is the ultimate test of mind and body. We try to push the limits of our own physiology by running faster and longer. In training at the edge of our capabilities, we walk a fine line, trying to balance the chance at a break through with the perils of break down and injury. The marathon itself exemplifies the need for this balance more than any other race because of its length."

BRIAN CLAS, WINNER OF THE 2000 PHILADELPHIA MARATHON

"Success is 90 percent physical and 10 percent mental. But never underestimate the power of that 10 percent."

TOM FLEMING IN *JOAN SAMUELSON'S RUNNING FOR WOMEN*

"There's not a better feeling than when you have found that moment of balance and harmony when both running and life come together. Then you know why you run and that you couldn't live without it."

JOAN BENOIT SAMUELSON, *RUNNING FOR WOMEN*

"You are tomorrow what you believe today."

GARY ELLIOTT, COACH TO ALLISON ROE

"You don't carry your groceries when you run, why should you carry your mental baggage with you? It'll still be there when you stop running."

DR. LINDA BUNKER IN *JOAN SAMUELSON'S RUNNING FOR WOMEN*

"It's a treat, being a long-distance runner, out in the world by yourself with not a soul to make you bad-tempered or tell you what to do or that there's a shop to break and enter a bit back from the next street."

ALAN SILLITOE, *THE LONELINESS OF THE LONG DISTANCE RUNNER*

———

"What marathon? Any marathon. Every marathon. It didn't much matter. It still doesn't matter. What counts is your desire—no, your need—to test yourself."

JOEL HOMER, *MARATHONS: THE ULTIMATE CHALLENGE*

———

"Why couldn't Pheidippides have died at 20 miles?"

FRANK SHORTER IN *RUNNING WITH THE LEGENDS*

"Remember then if there's one hard and fast rule in the distance-running game, it's that there are no hard and fast rules, no panaceas, no magic formulas for putting it all together. To be able to take good advice and adapt it to your needs—that's the trick."

ROY KISSEN, "FIFTEEN QUICK TRAINING TIPS," IN *THE COMPLETE RUNNER*, VOL. 2

"But if the dance of the run isn't fun, then discover another dance, because without fun the good of the run is undone, and a suffering runner always quits sooner or later."

FRED ROHE, *THE ZEN OF RUNNING*

"I'm never going to run another marathon."

OPRAH WINFREY IN *THE QUOTABLE RUNNER*

"Hurry slowly. Be dedicated and disciplined and work hard, but take your time. Move ahead, but be patient."

GRETE WAITZ IN *RUNNING WITH THE LEGENDS*

"I run into being and becoming and having been. Into feeling and seeing and hearing. Into all those senses by which I know the world that God made, and me in it. Into understanding why a Being whose reason to exist is 'to be' should have made me to His image."

GEORGE SHEEHAN, *RUNNING AND BEING*

"There is no secret to this marathon game. You must think clean, live clean, obey the laws of nature and God. You may fool the people for a time if you don't obey these rules, but you won't fool God, and if you don't live clean you will ultimately have to pay, both here and in the life hereafter."

JOHNNY MILES, WINNER OF THE 1926 BOSTON MARATHON, IN *BOSTON MARATHON* BY TOM DERDERIAN

"Being Great Runners is not the attainment we need. It is self-control. Without, ego forces us into ambition and the price of ambition is pain. Let's not be egotistical, let's take it easy."

FRED ROHE, *THE ZEN OF RUNNING*

"Our thoughts and beliefs are the blueprints from which we create our physical reality."

LORRAINE MOLLER IN *RUNNING WITH THE LEGENDS*

———————

"'Life,' said William James, 'is made in doing and suffering and creating.' It is all there in the marathon—the doing in training and the suffering in the race and, finally, the creating that comes in the tranquility of the aftermath."

GEORGE SHEEHAN IN *THE NEW YORK ROAD RUNNERS CLUB COMPLETE BOOK OF RUNNING AND FITNESS*

———————

"Competitive running is a metaphor for the unresting aspiration of the human spirit."

ROGER ROBINSON, *HEROES AND SPARROWS: A CELEBRATION OF RUNNING*

"As an athlete, when you least expect it, you may find yourself standing on the threshold of an accomplishment so monumental that it strikes fear into your soul. You must stand ready, at any moment, to face the unknown. You must be ready to walk boldly through the wall of uncertainty."

JOHN "THE PENGUIN" BINGHAM, *THE COURAGE TO START*

"We have only one life to live, and it passes by very quickly. So we'll go for it, and maybe see if it's possible. And if we don't make it, at least we'll know we gave it our best effort. That's all any of us can do."

UTA PIPPIG IN *RUNNING WITH THE LEGENDS*

"Not the race, but the runner. The enemy, as always, is within."

GEORGE SHEEHAN, *RUNNING AND BEING*

"There's not a lot you can do about your normal ability, but there's a hell of a lot you can do about the way you apply it."

DAVE MOORCROFT, IN *EVERY RUNNER'S COMPANION*

"Running is about defeating death, not inflicting it."

JOHN JEROME, *THE ELEMENTS OF EFFORT*

"If he could conquer the weakness, the cowardice in himself, he would not worry about the rest; it would come. Training was a rite of purification; from it came speed, strength. Racing was a rite of death; from it came knowledge."

JOHN L. PARKER, *ONCE A RUNNER*

"The weakest among us can become some kind of athlete, but only the strongest can survive as spectators."

GEORGE SHEEHAN, *DR. GEORGE SHEEHAN ON RUNNING*

"Now, here, you see, it takes all the running you can do, to keep in the same place."

THROUGH THE LOOKING GLASS BY LEWIS CARROLL

"Life consists partly in the tempering of ideals, to bring the finishing tape nearer, partly in a continual and restless reaching towards it."

ROGER BANNISTER, *THE FOUR MINUTE MILE*

"I've learned that finishing a marathon—or even five or ten miles, if that's as far as you choose to go—isn't just an athletic achievement. It's a state of mind; a state of mind that says anything is possible."

JOHN HANC, *THE ESSENTIAL RUNNER*

"For most of us, a marathon is less a race than a survival test. The big question before a shorter race is 'How fast will I finish?' The big one before a marathon is 'Will I finish at all?'"

JOE HENDERSON

"When you have the running spirit, you look forward to life. I firmly believe that I wouldn't have lived as long or as happily as I have without running."

MAX POPPER IN *THE ESSENTIAL RUNNER*

"... the marathoner is the man and woman who never stops running. To cross the finish line is only to cross another starting line. The challenge is the race and the race never ends."

JOEL HOMER, *MARATHONS: THE ULTIMATE CHALLENGE*

"Where have all the heroes gone? They've gone with the simplicities and the pieties and the easy answers of another era. Our lack of heroes is an indication of the maturity of our age. A realization that every man has come into his own and has the capability of making a success out of his life. But also that this success rests with having the courage and endurance and, above all, the will to become the person you are, however peculiar that may be. Then you will be able to say, 'I have found my hero and he is me.'"

GEORGE SHEEHAN IN *THE COMPLETE BOOK OF RUNNING*

"When you get down to it, it's the people you get to meet. If I want to tell you the most about a person in the fewest words simply say, 'He's a runner.'"

PAUL FETSCHER, WARREN STREET SOCIAL AND ATHLETIC CLUB

"A runner is a runner. We all hurt the same when we run this far, this fast. He told himself that, but he wasn't sure he believed it."

BRUCE TUCKMAN, *THE LONG ROAD TO BOSTON*

"I run with my head, my heart and my guts. . . ."

STEVE JONES IN *RUNNING WITH THE LEGENDS*

"Running is a way of life for me, just like brushing my teeth. If I don't run for a few days, I feel as if something's been stolen from me."

JOHN A. KELLY IN *BOSTON* BY HAL HIGDON

———

"To run is to live. Everything else is just waiting."

MARK HANSON IN *THE COMPLETE BOOK OF RUNNING*

———

"If you want to know the runner you really are, not the one you once were or imagine yourself becoming, run a marathon. Any marathon will do."

JOE HENDERSON, *MARATHON TRAINING*

"The spirit and the flesh go together like the night and the day. They blend into one another. The will is the catalyst that merges them together into one during those brief moments when we go all out."

BRUCE TUCKMAN, *THE LONG ROAD TO BOSTON*

———•◦•———

"I was really ready and didn't get the breaks. That's life . . . you work hard for just a few chances."

STEVE PREFONTAINE IN *PRE* BY TOM JORDAN

———•◦•———

"Steve Prefontaine was the type of runner that hated to lose, but wasn't afraid to lose. What I admire about this attitude is the willingness to take risks and put yourself in a position to achieve greatness even when the odds may be against you. In other words, you may fall, but at least you gave yourself a chance to win."

BRIAN CLAS, NEW YORK, NY, WINNER OF THE 2000 PHILADELPHIA MARATHON

"Just doing it is what matters. Don't put pressure on yourself to become faster, and don't let anyone else push your pace unless you want him or her to."

KATHRINE SWITZER, RUNNING AND WALKING FOR WOMEN OVER 40

"Some people create with words or with music or with brush and paints. I like to make something beautiful. When I run, I like to make people stop and say, 'I've never seen anyone run like that before.' It's more than just a race, it's style. It's doing something better than anyone else. It's being creative."

STEVE PREFONTAINE IN PRE BY TOM JORDAN

"The marathon is an art; the marathoner is an artist."

COACH KIYOSHI NAKAMURA IN RUNNING WITH THE LEGENDS

"Finishing a marathon forces everyone to bring mind and body together and to reach for extra resources from the power of the human spirit."

JEFF GALLOWAY, *JEFF GALLOWAY'S TRAINING JOURNAL*

"Marathoners can say of their finishes what pilots say of their landings. Any you can walk away from is good enough to let you take a small measure of pride along with the big dose of humility."

JOE HENDERSON, *MARATHON TRAINING*

"I have this marathon a little bit in my heart."

UTA PIPPIG, GERMAN MARATHON CHAMPION, OF THE BOSTON MARATHON, IN *BOSTON MARATHON* BY TOM DERDERIAN

"I could lose and live with the knowledge that I'd given 120 percent, given it all, if I'd been beaten by a guy who came up with 130 percent. But to lose because I'd let it go to the last lap . . . I'd always wonder whether I might have broken away. . . ."

STEVE PREFONTAINE IN *PRE* BY TOM JORDAN

"And this long-distance running lark is the best of all, because it makes me think so good that I learn things even better than when I'm on my bed at night."

ALAN SILLITOE, *THE LONELINESS OF THE LONG DISTANCE RUNNER*

"Family and friends are perplexed by this powerful desire to run some 26 miles again, because for decades I've had debilitating back pain from an injury I acquired by training for marathons. But those who have run the race hear its siren call and understand firsthand how psychology trumps physiology."

JEROME GROOPMAN IN *THE BOSTON MARATHON* BY JOE FALLS

———◆·◆·◆———

"The most important reason to run a marathon is for yourself. You should not start training to please your significant other, to impress your boss, or to prove to your friends or family that you are not a wimp. But there is no denying that your marathon training and race will have an effect on others."

GORDON BAKOULIS BLOCH, *HOW TO TRAIN FOR AND RUN YOUR BEST MARATHON*

"In the greater game we strive not for winning, but to extend our personal boundaries of who we are and what we can be, not as much to become faster as to become more, not to punish but to enjoy, not to beat someone else, but to become the best we can be, not to destroy others, but to create ourselves in motion as a celebration of our creaturehood. True excellence is achieved only in playing the greater game."

LORRAINE MOLLER IN *BOSTON MARATHON* BY TOM DERDERIAN

"He ran because it grounded him in basics. There was both life and death in it; it was unadulterated by media hype, trivial cares, political meddling. He suspected it kept him from that most real variety of schizophrenia that the republic is currently sprouting like mushrooms on a stump."

JOHN L. PARKER, *ONCE A RUNNER*

"If you have any doubts about doing the marathon, put them away. It's an awesome experience. Live every day to its fullest because you never know when it's gonna be your last."

EDDIE FELIX, AFTER COMPLETING THE LOS ANGELES MARATHON, MARCH 2001

———•·•·•———

"The marathon. How an average runner becomes more than average."

ONE OF NEW BALANCE'S TOP 10 REASONS TO RUN A MARATHON

———•·•·•———

"When I finish a run, every part of me is smiling."

JEFF GALLOWAY, *JEFF GALLOWAY'S TRAINING JOURNAL*

"It was not an immediate love affair between me and the marathon."

JOHN A. KELLY, IN "50 YEARS OF MARATHONING," IN
THE COMPLETE MARATHONER

"Marathon fever. Sooner or later it's gonna get you."

JOEL HOMER, *MARATHONS: THE ULTIMATE CHALLENGE*

"The marathon never ceases to be a race of joy, a race of wonder."

HAL HIGDON, *MARATHON: THE ULTIMATE TRAINING GUIDE*

"It is not the runner, but those impersonating the runner, who is at hazard."

GEORGE SHEEHAN, *RUNNING AND BEING*

"The distance that captivates one person's imagination repels another."

RICHARD BENYO, *THE MASTERS OF THE MARATHON*

"Man is so made, that whenever anything fires his soul, impossibilities vanish."

LA FONTAINE

"My only principle is to run for the pure running of it."

RICK TRUJILLO, MULTIPLE PIKE'S PEAK MARATHON WINNER, IN
MARATHONS: THE ULTIMATE CHALLENGE

"Work is anything a body has to do. Play is anything a body doesn't have to do."

MARK TWAIN

"There is a mighty thin line between being a hero and being an idiot."

KELLY SMITH, LEAGUE CITY, TEXAS

"Winners have no monopoly on incentive or satisfaction, and runners know better than anyone that the heroes and the sparrows really are equal."

ROGER ROBINSON, *HEROES AND SPARROWS: A CELEBRATION OF RUNNING*

"I am fighting God. Fighting the limitations He gave me. Fighting the pain. Fighting the unfairness. Fighting all the evil in me and the world. And I will not give in. I will conquer this hill, and I will conquer it alone."

GEORGE SHEEHAN, *RUNNING AND BEING*

"If you are going to win any battle you have to do one thing. You have to make the mind run the body. Never let the body tell the mind what to do. The body will always give up. It is always tired morning, noon and night. But the body is never tired if the mind is not tired. You've always got to make the mind take over and keep going."

GEORGE S. PATTON

———————

"Keep knocking, and the joy inside will eventually open a window and look out to see who's there."

RUMI

———————

"When you come to the end of your rope, tie a knot and hang on."

ANONYMOUS

"It doesn't matter how slow you go, as long as you do not stop."

LAOTZU

———

"If you can make your heart and nerve and sinew serve your turn long after they are done, and so hold on when there is nothing in you, except the will that says to them 'hold on.'"

RUDYARD KIPLING

———

"After the race, I mused on marathon running . . . and how it provides males with insight into another exception, the experience of childbirth. In both cases, marked agony and exhaustion are subsumed by such lasting gratification that you are moved to repeat the process."

JEROME GROOPMAN IN *THE BOSTON MARATHON*, BY JOE FALLS

"Marathoning. The triumph of desire over reason."

ONE OF NEW BALANCE'S TOP 10 REASONS TO RUN A MARATHON

"Life's a brief lightning flash; great joy to him who grasps it in time."

NIKOS KAZANTZAKIS

"If you can find meaning in the type of running you need to do to stay on this team, chances are you can find meaning in another absurd pastime. Life."

ROBERT TOWNE, SCREENPLAY FOR *PRE*

Bibliography

Anderson, Bob. *The Complete Runner, vol. 2.* Mountain View, CA: Runners World Books, 1982.

Audain, Anne and John L. Parker, Jr. *Uncommon Heart.* Tallahassee, FL: Cedarwinds Publishing, 2000.

Bakoulis, Gordon and Candace Karv. *The Running Times Guide to Breakthrough Running.* Champaign, IL: Human Kinetics, 2000.

Bannister, Roger. *The Four-Minute Mile.* New York: The Lyons Press, 1981.

Barrett, Thomas and Robert Morrissey, Jr. *Marathon Runners.* New York: Julian Messner, 1981.

Benoit, Joan, with Sally Baker. *Running Tide.* New York: Knopf, 1987.

Benyo, Richard. *Making the Marathon Your Event.* New York: Random House, 1992.

—. *The Masters of the Marathon.* New York: Atheneum, 1983.

Bingham, John. *The Courage to Start.* New York: Simon & Schuster, 1999.

Bloch, Gordon Bakoulis. *How to Train for and Run Your Best Marathon.* New York: Simon & Schuster, 1993.

Bloom, Marc. *The Marathon: What It Takes to Go the Distance.* New York: Holf Rinehart & Winston, 1981.

Burfoot, Amby. *Runner's World Complete Book of Running.* Emmaus, PA: Rodale Press, 1997.

Chinmoy, Sri. *Emil Zatopek: Earth's Tearing Cry and Heaven's Bearing Smile.* Jamaica, NY: Agni Press, 1980.

Cooper, Pamela. *The American Marathon.* Syracuse, NY: Syracuse University Press, 1998.

Cross, Dolores E. *Breaking Through the Wall.* Chicago, IL: Third World Press, 2000.

DeMar, Clarence. *Marathon: The Clarence DeMar Story.* Tallahassee, FL: Cedarwinds Publishing, 1992.

Derderian, Tom. *Boston Marathon: The First Century of the World's Premier Running Event.* Champaign, IL: Human Kinetics, 1994.

Elliott, Richard. *The Competitive Edge.* NJ: Prentice Hall, 1984.

Fallls, Joe. *The Boston Marathon.* New York: Macmillan Publishing, 1977.

Fixx, James F. *The Complete Book of Running.* New York: Random House, 1977.

Galloway, Jeff. *Galloway's Book on Running.* Bolinas, CA: Shelter Publications, 1984.

—. *Jeff Galloway's Training Journal.* Atlanta, GA: Phidippides Publication, 1998.

—. *Marathon.* Atlanta, GA: Phidippides Publication, 2000.

Gambaccini, Peter. *The New York City Marathon: Twenty-Five Years.* New York: Rizzoli Books, 1993.

Greenwald, Matt. *The Smart Runner's Handbook.* Washington, D.C.: Open Road Publishing, 1995.

Hanc, John. *The Essential Marathoner: A Concise Guide to the Race of Your Life.* New York: The Lyons Press, 1996.

—. *The Essential Runner: A Concise Guide to the Basics for All Runners.* New York: The Lyons Press, 1994.

Harteis, Richard. *Marathon: A Story of Endurance and Friendship.* New York: W. W. Norton, 1989.

Henderson, Joe, ed. *The Complete Marathoner.* Mountain View, CA: World Publications, 1978.

—. *Jog, Run, Race.* Mountain View, CA: World Publications, 1977.

—. *Marathon Training: The Proven 100-Day Program for Success.* Champaign, IL: Human Kinetics, 1997.

—. *Run Farther, Run Faster.* Mountain View, CA: World Publications, 1979.

Higdon, Hal. *Boston: A Century of Running.* Emmaus, PA: Rodale Press, 1995.

—. *Marathon: The Ultimate Training Guide.* Emmaus, PA: Rodale Press, 1999.

—.*The Marathoners.* New York: G. P. Putnam's Sons, 1980.

Homer, Joel. *Marathons: The Ultimate Challenge.* Garden City, NY: Tree Communications/Doubleday/Dolphin, 1979.

Hosler, Ray, ed. *Boston: America's Oldest Marathon.* Mountain View, CA: Anderson World, 1980.

Jerome, John. *The Elements of Effort.* Halcottville, NY: Breakaway Books, 1997.

Jordan, Tom. *Pre: The Story of America's Greatest Running Legend Steve Prefontaine.* Emmaus, PA: Rodale Press, 1977.

Kislevitz, Gail Waesche. *First Marathons: Personal Encounters with the 26.2-Mile Monster.* Halcottville, NY: Breakaway Books, 1998.

Kostrubala, Thaddeus. *The Joy of Running.* New York: L.B. Lippincott Co., 1976.

Kuehls, Dave. *4 Months to a 4 Hour Marathon.* New York: Berkley Publishing Group, 1998.

Lebow, Fred and Gloria Averbuch. *The New York Road Runners Club Complete Book of Running and Fitness.* New York: Random House, 1998.

Lovesey, Peter. *Five Kings of Distance.* New York: St. Martin's Press, 1981.

Moore, Kenny. *Best Efforts.* Tallahassee, FL: Cedarwinds Publishing, 1982.

Osmun, Mark. *The Honolulu Marathon.* New York: J.B. Lippincott, 1979.

Parker, John L. *Once a Runner.* Tallahassee, FL: Cedarwinds Publishing, 1978.

Parker, John L. *Runners and Other Dreamers.* Tallahassee, FL: Cedarwinds Publishing, 1989.

Robinson, Roger. *Heroes and Sparrows: A Celebration of Running.* Southwestern Publishing, 1986.

Roe, Allison and Gary Elliott. *Every Runner's Companion.* (TO COME)

Rogers, Bill and Joe Concannon. *Marathoning.* New York: Simon & Schuster, 1980.

Rohe, Fred. *The Zen of Running.* New York: Random House, 1974.

Runner's World Magazine. *The Boston Marathon.* Mountain View, CA: World Publications, 1974.

Salazar, Alberto and Lovett, Rick. *Alberto Salazar's Guide to Running.* Blacklick, OH: Ragged Mountain Press/McGraw-Hill, 2001.

Samuelson, Joan Benoit and Gloria Averbuch. *Joan Samuelson's Running for Women.* Emmaus, PA: Rodale Press, 1995.

Sandrock, Michael. *Running with the Legends.* Champaign, IL: Human Kinetics, 1996.

Sheehan, George. *Dr. Sheehan on Running.* Mountain View, CA: World Publications, 1975.

—. *Personal Best.* Emmaus, PA: Rodale Press, 1989.

—. *Running and Being.* Red Bank, NJ: The George Sheehan Trust, 1978.

Sillitoe, Alan. *The Loneliness of the Long-Distance Runner.* New York: Knopf, 1965.

Steffny, Manfred, trans. by George Beinhorn. *Marathoning.* Mountain View, CA: World Publications, 1977.

Switzer, Kathrine. *Running and Walking for Women Over 40.* New York: St. Martin's Press, 1998.

Tuckman, Bruce W. *The Long Road to Boston.* Tallahassee, FL: Cedarwinds Publishing, 1988.

Will-Weber, Mark. *The Quotable Runner.* Halcottville, NY: Breakaway Books, 1995.

Index